MznLnx

Missing Links Exam Preps

Exam Prep for

Modeling the Dynamics of Life:Calculus and Probability for Life Scientists

Adler, 2nd Edition

The MznLnx Exam Prep is your link from the texbook and lecture to your exams.
The MznLnx Exam Preps are unauthorized and comprehensive reviews of your textbooks.

All material provided by MznLnx and Rico Publications (c) 2010
Textbook publishers and textbook authors do not particpate in or contribute to these reviews.

MznLnx

Rico
Publications

Exam Prep for Modeling the Dynamics of Life:Calculus and Probability for Life Scientists
2nd Edition
Adler

Publisher: Raymond Houge
Assistant Editor: Michael Rouger
Text and Cover Designer: Lisa Buckner
Marketing Manager: Sara Swagger
Project Manager, Editorial Production: Jerry Emerson
Art Director: Vernon Lowerui

Product Manager: Dave Mason
Editorial Assitant: Rachel Guzmanji
Pedagogy: Debra Long
Cover Image: Jim Reed/Getty Images
Text and Cover Printer: City Printing, Inc.
Compositor: Media Mix, Inc.

(c) 2010 Rico Publications
ALL RIGHTS RESERVED. No part of this work
covered by the copyright may be reproduced or
used in any form or by an means--graphic, electronic,
or mechanical, including photocopying, recording,
taping, Web distribution, information storage, and
retrieval systems, or in any other manner--without the
written permission of the publisher.

Printed in the United States
ISBN:

For more information about our products, contact us at:
Dave.Mason@RicoPublications.com

For permission to use material from this text or
product, submit a request online to:
Dave.Mason@RicoPublications.com

Contents

CHAPTER 1
Introduction to Discrete-Time Dynamical Systems — 1

CHAPTER 2
Limits and Derivatives — 15

CHAPTER 3
Applications of Derivatives and Dynamical Systems — 31

CHAPTER 4
Differential Equations, Integrals, and Their Applications — 45

CHAPTER 5
Analysis of Autonomous Differential Equations — 59

CHAPTER 6
Probability Theory and Descriptive Statistics — 67

CHAPTER 7
Probability Models — 76

CHAPTER 8
Introduction to Statistical Reasoning — 86

ANSWER KEY — 92

TO THE STUDENT

COMPREHENSIVE

The *MznLnx* Exam Prep series is designed to help you pass your exams. Editors at MznLnx review your textbooks and then prepare these practice exams to help you master the textbook material. Unlike study guides, workbooks, and practice tests provided by the texbook publisher and textbook authors, *MznLnx* gives you **all** of the material in each chapter in exam form, not just samples, so you can be sure to nail your exam.

MECHANICAL

The MznLnx Exam Prep series creates exams that will help you learn the subject matter as well as test you on your understanding. Each question is designed to help you master the concept. Just working through the exams, you gain an understanding of the subject--its a simple mechanical process that produces success.

INTEGRATED STUDY GUIDE AND REVIEW

MznLnx is not just a set of exams designed to test you, its also a comprehensive review of the subject content. Each exam question is also a review of the concept, making sure that you will get the answer correct without having to go to other sources of material. You learn as you go! Its the easiest way to pass an exam.

HUMOR

Studying can be tedious and dry. MznLnx's instructional design includes moderate humor within the exam questions on occassion, to break the tedium and revitalize the brain

Chapter 1. Introduction to Discrete-Time Dynamical Systems 1

1. In computer science and information science, _____ could also be a method or an algorithm. Again, an example will illustrate: There are systems of counting, as with Roman numerals, and various systems for filing papers, or catalogues, and various library systems, of which the Dewey Decimal _____ is an example. This still fits with the definition of components which are connected together (in this case in order to facilitate the flow of information.)
   a. BIBO stability
   b. BDDC
   c. 15 theorem
   d. System

2. In mathematics and its applications, a _____ system is a system for assigning an n-tuple of numbers or scalars to each point in an n-dimensional space. This concept is part of the theory of manifolds. 'Scalars' in many cases means real numbers, but, depending on context, can mean complex numbers or elements of some other commutative ring.
   a. Spherical coordinate system
   b. Cylindrical coordinate system
   c. Coordinate
   d. 15 theorem

3. _____ is the change in population over time, and can be quantified as the change in the number of individuals in a population using 'per unit time' for measurement. The term _____ can technically refer to any species, but almost always refers to humans, and it is often used informally for the more specific demographic term _____ rate , and is often used to refer specifically to the growth of the population of the world.

   Simple models of _____ include the Malthusian Growth Model and the logistic model.

   a. BIBO stability
   b. Population growth
   c. 15 theorem
   d. BDDC

4. The terms '_____' and 'independent variable' are used in similar but subtly different ways in mathematics and statistics as part of the standard terminology in those subjects. They are used to distinguish between two types of quantities being considered, separating them into those available at the start of a process and those being created by it, where the latter (dependent variables) are dependent on the former (independent variables.)

   In traditional calculus, a function is defined as a relation between two terms called variables because their values vary.

Chapter 1. Introduction to Discrete-Time Dynamical Systems

a. 15 theorem
b. BDDC
c. Dependent variable
d. BIBO stability

5. In mathematics, the _____ (or replacement set) of a given function is the set of 'input' values for which the function is defined. For instance, the _____ of cosine would be all real numbers, while the _____ of the square root would be only numbers greater than or equal to 0 (ignoring complex numbers in both cases.) In a representation of a function in a xy Cartesian coordinate system, the _____ is represented on the x axis (or abscissa.)
a. 15 theorem
b. Domain
c. BIBO stability
d. BDDC

6. The terms 'dependent variable' and '_____' are used in similar but subtly different ways in mathematics and statistics as part of the standard terminology in those subjects. They are used to distinguish between two types of quantities being considered, separating them into those available at the start of a process and those being created by it, where the latter (dependent variables) are dependent on the former (independent variables.)

In traditional calculus, a function is defined as a relation between two terms called variables because their values vary.

a. AUSM
b. ALGOR
c. ACTRAN
d. Independent variable

7. In mathematics, the _____ of a function is the set of all 'output' values produced by that function. Sometimes it is called the image, or more precisely, the image of the domain of the function. If a function is a surjection then its _____ is equal to its codomain.
a. Piecewise-defined function
b. Constant function
c. Surjective
d. Range

8. The _____ is a test to determine if a relation or its graph is a function or not. For a relation or graph to be a function, it can have at most a single y-value for each x-value. Thus, a vertical line drawn at any x-position on the graph of a function will intersect the graph at most once.

a. BDDC
b. 15 theorem
c. BIBO stability
d. Vertical line test

9. In mathematics, the _____ of a function y = f(x) is a function that, in some fashion, 'undoes' the effect of f The _____ of f is denoted f^{-1}. The statements y=f(x) and x=f^{-1}(y) are equivalent.
a. AUSM
b. ACTRAN
c. Inverse
d. ALGOR

10. In mathematics, if f is a function from A to B then an _____ for f is a function in the opposite direction, from B to A, with the property that a round trip (a composition) from A to B to A (or from B to A to B) returns each element of the initial set to itself. Thus, if an input x into the function f produces an output y, then inputting y into the _____ f^{-1} (read f inverse, not to be confused with exponentiation) produces the output x. Not every function has an inverse; those that do are called invertible.
a. Augustin-Jean Fresnel
b. Aristotle
c. Inverse function
d. Augustin Louis Cauchy

11. In mathematics, the _____ is a test used to determine if a function is injective, surjective or bijective.

Suppose there is a function f : X → Y with a graph., and you have a horizontal line of X x Y :
$y_0 \in Y, \{(x, y_0) : x \in X\} = (X \times y_0)$.

- If the function is injective, then it can be visualized as one whose graph is never intersected by any horizontal line more than once.
- If and only if f is surjective, any horizontal line will intersect the graph at least at one point (when the horizontal line is in the codomain.)
- If f is bijective, any horizontal line will intersect the graph at exactly one point.

This test is also used to find whether or not the inverse of the function is indeed a function as well. This is due to the reflective properties of the function over y=x.

a. 15 theorem
b. BDDC
c. BIBO stability
d. Horizontal line test

12. If a function has an integral, it is said to be integrable. The function for which the integral is calculated is called the _____. The region over which a function is being integrated is called the domain of integration.
    a. Integrand
    b. Integral test for convergence
    c. Integration by parts
    d. Order of integration

13. A _____ is perfectly round geometrical object in three-dimensional space, such as the shape of a round ball. Like a circle in two dimensions, a perfect _____ is completely symmetrical around its center, with all points on the surface lying the same distance r from the center point. This distance r is known as the radius of the _____.
    a. North pole
    b. Tangent line
    c. Sphere
    d. Minimal surface

14. _____ is how much exposed area an object has. It is expressed in square units. If an object has flat faces, its _____ can be calculated by adding together the areas of its faces.
    a. Vector area
    b. Surface area
    c. Plane curve
    d. Lipschitz domain

15. The _____ of any solid, liquid, plasma, vacuum or theoretical object is how much three-dimensional space it occupies, often quantified numerically. One-dimensional figures (such as lines) and two-dimensional shapes (such as squares) are assigned zero _____ in the three-dimensional space. _____ is commonly presented in units such as mL or cm^3 (milliliters or cubic centimeters.)
    a. Vector potential
    b. Volume
    c. Dirac equation
    d. Klein-Gordon equation

16. _____ is a type of motion in which the velocity of an object changes equal amounts in equal time periods. An example of an object having _____ would be a ball rolling down a ramp. The object picks up velocity as it goes down the ramp with equal changes in time.

a. ACTRAN
b. Uniform Acceleration
c. ALGOR
d. AUSM

17. is called the proportionality constant or _____.

- If an object travels at a constant speed, then the distance traveled is proportional to the time spent travelling, with the speed being the _____.

- The circumference of a circle is proportional to its diameter, with the _____ equal to π.

- On a map drawn to scale, the distance between any two points on the map is proportional to the distance between the two locations that the points represent, with the _____ being the scale of the map.

- The force acting on a certain object due to gravity is proportional to the object's mass; the _____ between the the mass and the force is known as gravitational acceleration.

Since

$$y = kx$$

is equivalent to

$$x = \left(\frac{1}{k}\right) y,$$

it follows that if y is proportional to x, with (nonzero) proportionality constant k, then x is also proportional to y with proportionality constant 1/k.

If y is proportional to x, then the graph of y as a function of x will be a straight line passing through the origin with the slope of the line equal to the _____: it corresponds to linear growth.

a. BDDC
b. Constant of proportionality
c. 15 theorem
d. Reduction

18. _____ is used to describe the steepness, incline, gradient, or grade of a straight line. A higher _____ value indicates a steeper incline. The _____ is defined as the ratio of the 'rise' divided by the 'run' between two points on a line, or in other words, the ratio of the altitude change to the horizontal distance between any two points on the line.

a. 15 theorem
b. Sequence
c. Y-intercept
d. Slope

19. A _____ is an algebraic equation in which each term is either a constant or the product of a constant and (the first power of) a single variable. Linear equations can have one, two, three or more variables. Linear equations occur with great regularity in applied mathematics.

a. Quartic function
b. Cubic function
c. Linear equation
d. Quadratic formula

20. In coordinate geometry, the _____ is the y-value of the point where the graph of a function or relation intercepts the y-axis of the coordinate system.

In other words, the _____ of a function is the y-value of the point at which it intersects the line x=0 (the y-axis.) Thus, if the function is specified in form y = f(x), the _____ is easy to find by calculating f.

a. Sequence
b. Y-intercept
c. 15 theorem
d. Slope

21. In mathematics, a _____ is a function which preserves the given order. This concept first arose in calculus, and was later generalized to the more abstract setting of order theory.

In calculus, a function f defined on a subset of the real numbers with real values is called monotonic (also monotonically increasing or non-decreasing), if for all x and y such that x >≤ y one has f(x) >≤ f(y), so f preserves the order.

a. Pettis integral
b. Pseudo-differential operator
c. Monotonic function
d. 15 theorem

22. In chemistry, _____ is the measure of how much of a given substance there is mixed with another substance. This can apply to any sort of chemical mixture, but most frequently the concept is limited to homogeneous solutions, where it refers to the amount of solute in the solvent.

To concentrate a solution, one must add more solute, or reduce the amount of solvent (for instance, by selective evaporation.)

   a. Concentration
   b. BIBO stability
   c. BDDC
   d. 15 theorem

23. In infinitesimal calculus, a _____ is traditionally an infinitesimally small change in a variable. For example, if x is a variable, then a change in the value of x is often denoted Δx (or δx when this change is considered to be small.) The _____ dx represents such a change, but is infinitely small.
   a. Dirichlet integral
   b. Local maximum
   c. The Method of Mechanical Theorems
   d. Differential

24. A _____ is a mathematical equation for an unknown function of one or several variables that relates the values of the function itself and of its derivatives of various orders. they play a prominent role in engineering, physics, economics and other disciplines.

A simplified real world example of a _____ is modeling the acceleration of a ball falling through the air (considering only gravity and air resistance.)

   a. Phase line
   b. Caloric polynomial
   c. Structural stability
   d. Differential equation

25. _____ typically refers to a state lacking order or predictability. In ancient Greece, it referred to the initial state of the universe, and, by extension, space, darkness, or an abyss. In modern English, it is used in classical studies with this original meaning; in mathematics and science to refer to a very specific kind of unpredictability; and informally to mean a state of confusion.

a. 15 theorem
b. BIBO stability
c. BDDC
d. Chaos

26. In mathematical analysis, the _____ states that for each value between the least upper bound and greatest lower bound of the image of a continuous function there is a corresponding value in its domain mapping to the original. _____

- Version I. The _____ states the following: If the function y = f(x) is continuous on the interval [a, b], and u is a number between f(a) and f(b), then there is a c ∈ [a, b] such that f(c) = u.

- Version II. Suppose that I is an interval [a, b] in the real numbers R and that f : I → R is a continuous function. Then the image set f(I) is also an interval, and either it contains [f(a), f(b)], or it contains [f(b), f(a)]; that is,

    f(I) ⊇ [f(a), f(b)], or f(I) ⊇ [f(b), f(a)].

It is frequently stated in the following equivalent form: Suppose that f : [a, b] → R is continuous and that u is a real number satisfying f(a) < u < f(b) or f(a) > u > f(b).) Then for some c ∈ [a, b], f(c) = u.

This captures an intuitive property of continuous functions: given f continuous on [1, 2], if f(1) = 3 and f(2) = 5 then f must take the value 4 somewhere between 1 and 2.

a. ACTRAN
b. ALGOR
c. AUSM
d. Intermediate Value Theorem

27. The _____ is a function in mathematics. The application of this function to a value x is written as exp(x). Equivalently, this can be written in the form e^x, where e is a mathematical constant, the base of the natural logarithm, which equals approximately 2.718281828, and is also known as Euler's number.
a. Integral part
b. Exponential function
c. Area hyperbolic functions
d. ACTRAN

Chapter 1. Introduction to Discrete-Time Dynamical Systems 9

28. In calculus, a branch of mathematics, the _____ is a measurement of how a function changes when its input changes. Loosely speaking, a _____ can be thought of as how much a quantity is changing at some given point. For example, the _____ of the position (or distance) of a vehicle with respect to time is the instantaneous velocity (respectively, instantaneous speed) at which the vehicle is traveling.

The process of finding a _____ is called differentiation. The fundamental theorem of calculus states that differentiation is the reverse process to integration.

   a. Semi-differentiability
   b. Bounded function
   c. Stationary phase approximation
   d. Derivative

29. The _____, formerly known as the hyperbolic logarithm, is the logarithm to the base e, where e is an irrational constant approximately equal to 2.718281828. It is also sometimes referred to as the Napierian logarithm, although the original meaning of this term is slightly different. In simple terms, the _____ of a number x is the power to which e would have to be raised to equal x -- for example the natural log of e itself is 1 because e^1 = e, while the _____ of 1 would be 0, since e^0 = 1.
   a. BIBO stability
   b. BDDC
   c. 15 theorem
   d. Natural logarithm

30. The natural logarithm, formerly known as the hyperbolic logarithm, is the logarithm to the _____, where e is an irrational constant approximately equal to 2.718281828. It is also sometimes referred to as the Napierian logarithm, although the original meaning of this term is slightly different. In simple terms, the natural logarithm of a number x is the power to which e would have to be raised to equal x -- for example the natural log of e itself is 1 because e^1 = e, while the natural logarithm of 1 would be 0, since e^0 = 1.
   a. Base e
   b. 15 theorem
   c. BIBO stability
   d. BDDC

31. The _____ of a quantity whose value decreases with time is the interval required for the quantity to decay to half of its initial value. The concept originated in describing how long it takes atoms to undergo radioactive decay but also applies in a wide variety of other situations.

The term '_____' dates to 1907.

a. 15 theorem
b. Half-life
c. BIBO stability
d. BDDC

32. In mathematics, in the field of ordinary differential equations, a non trivial solution to an ordinary differential equation

$$F(x, y, y', \ldots, y^{(n-1)}) = y^{(n)} \quad x \in [0, +\infty)$$

is called _____ if it has an infinite number of roots, otherwise it is called non-_____. The differential equation is called _____ if it has an _____ solution.

The differential equation

y" + y = 0

is _____ as sin(x) is a solution.

a. Exponential growth
b. Integrating factor
c. Inseparable differential equation
d. Oscillating

33. The _____ of an angle is the ratio of the length of the adjacent side to the length of the hypotenuse. In our case

$$\cos A = \frac{\text{adjacent}}{\text{hypotenuse}} = \frac{b}{h}.$$

The tangent of an angle is the ratio of the length of the opposite side to the length of the adjacent side. In our case

$$\tan A = \frac{\text{opposite}}{\text{adjacent}} = \frac{a}{b}.$$

The remaining three functions are best defined using the above three functions.

a. Trigonometric functions
b. Sine integral
c. Trigonometric
d. Cosine

34. The _____ of an angle is the ratio of the length of the opposite side to the length of the hypotenuse. In our case

$$\sin A = \frac{\text{opposite}}{\text{hypotenuse}} = \frac{a}{h}.$$

Note that this ratio does not depend on size of the particular right triangle chosen, as long as it contains the angle A, since all such triangles are similar.

The cosine of an angle is the ratio of the length of the adjacent side to the length of the hypotenuse.

a. Trigonometric functions
b. Trigonometric
c. Sine integral
d. Sine

35. Trigonometry is a branch of mathematics that deals with triangles, particularly those plane triangles in which one angle has 90 degrees (right triangles.) Trigonometry deals with relationships between the sides and the angles of triangles and with the _____ functions, which describe those relationships.

Trigonometry has applications in both pure mathematics and in applied mathematics, where it is essential in many branches of science and technology.

a. Trigonometric integrals
b. Sine
c. Trigonometric functions
d. Trigonometric

36. In mathematics, the _____ are functions of an angle. They are important in the study of triangles and modeling periodic phenomena, among many other applications. _____ are commonly defined as ratios of two sides of a right triangle containing the angle, and can equivalently be defined as the lengths of various line segments from a unit circle.

Chapter 1. Introduction to Discrete-Time Dynamical Systems

   a. Trigonometric functions
   b. Sine integral
   c. Trigonometric
   d. Trigonometric integrals

37. _____ is the magnitude of change in the oscillating variable, with each oscillation, within an oscillating system. For instance, sound waves are oscillations in atmospheric pressure and their amplitudes are proportional to the change in pressure during one oscillation. If the variable undergoes regular oscillations, and a graph of the system is drawn with the oscillating variable as the vertical axis and time as the horizontal axis, the _____ is visually represented by the vertical distance between the extrema of the curve.
   a. ACTRAN
   b. Amplitude
   c. AUSM
   d. ALGOR

38. In a totally ordered set all elements are mutually comparable, so such a set can have at most one minimal element and at most one maximal element. Then, due to mutual comparability, the minimal element will also be the least element and the maximal element will also be the greatest element. Thus in a totally ordered set we can simply use the terms minimum and _____.
   a. Nth term
   b. Maximum
   c. Leibniz rule
   d. Racetrack principle

39. In a totally ordered set all elements are mutually comparable, so such a set can have at most one minimal element and at most one maximal element. Then, due to mutual comparability, the minimal element will also be the least element and the maximal element will also be the greatest element. Thus in a totally ordered set we can simply use the terms _____ and maximum.
   a. Maximum
   b. Minimum
   c. Ghosts of departed quantities
   d. Nth term

40. In mathematics, an autonomous system or _____ is a system of ordinary differential equations which does not depend on the independent variable.

Many laws in physics, where the independent variable is usually assumed to be time, are expressed as autonomous systems because it is assumed the laws of nature which hold now are identical to those for any point in the past or future.

Autonomous systems are closely related to dynamical systems.

- a. Annihilator method
- b. Autonomous differential equation
- c. Integro-differential equation
- d. Algebraic differential equation

41. In geometry, the _____ (or simply the tangent) to a curve at a given point is the straight line that 'just touches' the curve at that point (in the sense explained more precisely below.) As it passes through the point of tangency, the _____ is 'going in the same direction' as the curve, and in this sense it is the best straight-line approximation to the curve at that point. The same definition applies to space curves and curves in n-dimensional Euclidean space.
    - a. North pole
    - b. Lie derivative
    - c. Minimal surface
    - d. Tangent line

42. A _____ officer is an officer of high military rank. The term or equivalent is used by nearly every country in the world. _____ can be used as a generic term for all grades of _____ officer, or it can specifically refer to a single rank that is just called _____.
    - a. General
    - b. BIBO stability
    - c. 15 theorem
    - d. BDDC

43. The _____ is a polynomial mapping of degree 2, often cited as an archetypal example of how complex, chaotic behaviour can arise from very simple non-linear dynamical equations. The map was popularized in a seminal 1976 paper by the biologist Robert May, in part as a discrete-time demographic model analogous to the logistic equation first created by Pierre François Verhulst. Mathematically, the _____ is written

$$(1) \qquad x_{n+1} = rx_n(1 - x_n)$$

where:

> x_n is a number between zero and one, and represents the population at year n, and hence x_0 represents the initial population (at year 0)
> r is a positive number, and represents a combined rate for reproduction and starvation.

a. 15 theorem
b. BIBO stability
c. BDDC
d. Logistic map

44. _____, the behaviour of a linear autonomous system around a critical point is a _____ if the following conditions are satisifed:

Each path converges to the critical as $t \to \infty$ (or as $t \to -\infty$.) Furthermore, each path approaches the point asymptotically through a line.

a. Node
b. Growth curve
c. Frobenius method
d. Laser diode rate equations

Chapter 2. Limits and Derivatives

1. A _____ of a curve is a line that (locally) intersects two points on the curve. The word secant comes from the Latin secare, for to cut.

It can be used to approximate the tangent to a curve, at some point P. If the secant to a curve is defined by two points, P and Q, with P fixed and Q variable, as Q approaches P along the curve, the direction of the secant approaches that of the tangent at P, assuming there is just one.

  a. Witch of Agnesi
  b. Curve
  c. Kappa curve
  d. Secant line

2. In geometry, the _____ (or simply the tangent) to a curve at a given point is the straight line that 'just touches' the curve at that point (in the sense explained more precisely below.) As it passes through the point of tangency, the _____ is 'going in the same direction' as the curve, and in this sense it is the best straight-line approximation to the curve at that point. The same definition applies to space curves and curves in n-dimensional Euclidean space.
  a. Tangent line
  b. North pole
  c. Lie derivative
  d. Minimal surface

3. In calculus, a branch of mathematics, the _____ is a measurement of how a function changes when its input changes. Loosely speaking, a _____ can be thought of as how much a quantity is changing at some given point. For example, the _____ of the position (or distance) of a vehicle with respect to time is the instantaneous velocity (respectively, instantaneous speed) at which the vehicle is traveling.

The process of finding a _____ is called differentiation. The fundamental theorem of calculus states that differentiation is the reverse process to integration.

  a. Derivative
  b. Bounded function
  c. Stationary phase approximation
  d. Semi-differentiability

4. In infinitesimal calculus, a _____ is traditionally an infinitesimally small change in a variable. For example, if x is a variable, then a change in the value of x is often denoted Δx (or δx when this change is considered to be small.) The _____ dx represents such a change, but is infinitely small.

Chapter 2. Limits and Derivatives

a. Differential
b. The Method of Mechanical Theorems
c. Dirichlet integral
d. Local maximum

5. In mathematics, the concept of a '_____' is used to describe the behavior of a function as its argument or input either 'gets close' to some point, or as the argument becomes arbitrarily large; or the behavior of a sequence's elements as their index increases indefinitely. Limits are used in calculus and other branches of mathematical analysis to define derivatives and continuity.

In formulas, _____ is usually abbreviated as lim

a. BDDC
b. 15 theorem
c. BIBO stability
d. Limit

6. _____ is used to describe the steepness, incline, gradient, or grade of a straight line. A higher _____ value indicates a steeper incline. The _____ is defined as the ratio of the 'rise' divided by the 'run' between two points on a line, or in other words, the ratio of the altitude change to the horizontal distance between any two points on the line.

a. Y-intercept
b. 15 theorem
c. Sequence
d. Slope

7. In mathematics, a (topological) _____ is defined as follows: let I be an interval of real numbers (i.e. a non-empty connected subset of $\mathbb{R}$); then a _____ γ is a continuous mapping $\gamma : I \to X$, where X is a topological space. The _____ γ is said to be simple if it is injective, i.e. if for all x, y in I, we have $\gamma(x) = \gamma(y) \implies x = y$. If I is a closed bounded interval $[a, b]$, we also allow the possibility $\gamma(a) = \gamma(b)$ (this convention makes it possible to talk about closed simple _____.)

a. Curve
b. Closed curve
c. Tractrix
d. Prolate cycloid

Chapter 2. Limits and Derivatives

8. A _____ is a mathematical equation for an unknown function of one or several variables that relates the values of the function itself and of its derivatives of various orders. they play a prominent role in engineering, physics, economics and other disciplines.

A simplified real world example of a _____ is modeling the acceleration of a ball falling through the air (considering only gravity and air resistance.)

   a. Differential equation
   b. Structural stability
   c. Phase line
   d. Caloric polynomial

9. A _____ is a statement of the meaning of a word or phrase. The term to be defined is known as the definiendum . The words which define it are known as the definiens .
   a. BIBO stability
   b. 15 theorem
   c. BDDC
   d. Definition

10. _____ is a type of motion in which the velocity of an object changes equal amounts in equal time periods. An example of an object having _____ would be a ball rolling down a ramp. The object picks up velocity as it goes down the ramp with equal changes in time.
    a. ACTRAN
    b. ALGOR
    c. Uniform Acceleration
    d. AUSM

11. In mathematics, a _____ is a function whose values do not vary and thus are constant. For example, if we have the function f(x) = 4, then f is constant since f maps any value to 4. More formally, a function f : A → B is a _____ if f(x) = f(y) for all x and y in A.
    a. Range
    b. Piecewise-defined function
    c. Surjective
    d. Constant function

12. In mathematics, an _____ is a function that always returns the same value that was used as its argument. In terms of equations, the function is given by f = x.

Formally, if M is a set, the _____ f on M is defined to be that function with domain and codomain M which satisfies

f = x for all elements x in M.

a. Onto
b. One-to-one
c. Identity function
d. One-to-one function

13. In mathematics, a _____ is any function which can be written as the ratio of two polynomial functions.

$$y = \frac{x^2 - 3x - 2}{x^2 - 4}$$

In the case of one variable, x, a _____ is a function of the form

$$f(x) = \frac{P(x)}{Q(x)}$$

where P and Q are polynomial function in x and Q is not the zero polynomial. The domain of f is the set of all points x for which the denominator Q(x) is not zero.

a. 15 theorem
b. BIBO stability
c. BDDC
d. Rational function

14. In physics, _____ is defined as the rate of change of position. it is vector physical quantity; both speed and direction are required to define it. In the SI (metric) system, it is measured in meters per second: (m/s) or ms^{-1}.

a. 15 theorem
b. BIBO stability
c. BDDC
d. Velocity

Chapter 2. Limits and Derivatives

15. Cantor defined two kinds of _____ numbers, the ordinal numbers and the cardinal numbers. Ordinal numbers may be identified with well-ordered sets, or counting carried on to any stopping point, including points after an _____ number have already been counted. Generalizing finite and the ordinary _____ sequences which are maps from the positive integers leads to mappings from ordinal numbers, and transfinite sequences.

   a. ACTRAN
   b. Infinite
   c. AUSM
   d. ALGOR

16. The _____, formerly known as the hyperbolic logarithm, is the logarithm to the base e, where e is an irrational constant approximately equal to 2.718281828. It is also sometimes referred to as the Napierian logarithm, although the original meaning of this term is slightly different. In simple terms, the _____ of a number x is the power to which e would have to be raised to equal x -- for example the natural log of e itself is 1 because e^1 = e, while the _____ of 1 would be 0, since e^0 = 1.

   a. BIBO stability
   b. 15 theorem
   c. BDDC
   d. Natural logarithm

17. In mathematics, a _____ is a function for which, intuitively, small changes in the input result in small changes in the output. Otherwise, a function is said to be discontinuous. A _____ with a continuous inverse function is called bicontinuous. An intuitive though imprecise (and inexact) idea of continuity is given by the common statement that a _____ is a function whose graph can be drawn without lifting the chalk from the blackboard.

   a. Continuous function
   b. Visual Calculus
   c. Hyperbolic angle
   d. Binomial series

18. In mathematics, the sign function is an odd mathematical function that extracts the sign of a real number. To avoid confusion with the sine function, this function is often called the _____ .

   In mathematical expressions the sign function is often represented as sgn.

   a. Hyperbolic tangent
   b. Signum function
   c. Heaviside step function
   d. Hyperbolic functions

19. The _____, H, also called the unit step function, is a discontinuous function whose value is zero for negative argument and one for positive argument. It seldom matters what value is used for H, since H is mostly used as a distribution. The function is used in the mathematics of control theory and signal processing to represent a signal that switches on at a specified time and stays switched on indefinitely.

   a. Hyperbolic functions
   b. Hyperbolic sine
   c. Heaviside step function
   d. Square root function

20. In mathematics, a _____ (or critical number) is a point on the domain of a function where:

   - one dimension: the derivative (or slope of the line when visualized) is equal to zero or a point where the function ceases to be differentiable.
   - in general: there are two distinct concepts: either the derivative (Jacobian) vanishes, or it is not of full rank (or, in either case, the function is not differentiable); these agree in one dimension.

Note that in one dimension, a critical value or critical number x of function f is the domain element at which the derivative is zero or undefined, whereas the associated ordered pair (x, y) is the _____. In higher dimensions a critical value is in the range whereas a _____ is in the domain.

There are two situations in which a point becomes a _____ of a function of one variable. The first of which is that the value of the first derivative is equal to zero.

   a. Multivariable calculus
   b. Total derivative
   c. Differentiation operator
   d. Critical point

21. A _____, in mathematics, is a polynomial function of the form $f(x) = ax^2 + bx + c$, where $a \neq 0$. The graph of a _____ is a parabola whose major axis is parallel to the y-axis.

The expression $ax^2 + bx + c$ in the definition of a _____ is a polynomial of degree 2 or a 2nd degree polynomial, because the highest exponent of x is 2.

   a. Leading coefficient
   b. Discriminant
   c. Resultant
   d. Quadratic function

Chapter 2. Limits and Derivatives

22. In elementary algebra, a _____ is a polynomial with two terms--the sum of two monomials--often bound by parenthesis or brackets when operated upon. It is the simplest kind of polynomial other than monomials.

- The _____ a² - b² can be factored as the product of two other binomials:

  a² - b² = (a + b)(a - b.)

  This is a special case of the more general formula:

  $$a^{n+1} - b^{n+1} = (a-b) \sum_{k=0}^{n} a^k b^{n-k}$$

- The product of a pair of linear binomials (ax + b) and (cx + d) is:

  (ax + b)(cx + d) = acx² + axd + bcx + bd.

- A _____ raised to the nth power, represented as

  (a + b)^n

  can be expanded by means of the _____ theorem or, equivalently, using Pascal's triangle. Taking a simple example, the perfect square _____ (p + q)² can be found by squaring the first digit, adding twice the product of the first and second digit and finally adding the square of the second digit, to give p² + 2pq + q².

a. Multinomial theorem
b. Binomial
c. Completing the square
d. Partial fractions

23. In mathematics, the _____ is an important formula giving the expansion of powers of sums. Its simplest version states that

$$(x+y)^n = \sum_{k=0}^{n} \binom{n}{k} x^{n-k} y^k \qquad (1)$$

for any real or complex numbers x and y, and any non-negative integer n. The binomial coefficient appearing in (1) may be defined in terms of the factorial function n!:

$$\binom{n}{k} = \frac{n!}{k!\,(n-k)!}.$$

For example, here are the cases where 2 ≤ n ≤ 5:

$$(x+y)^2 = x^2 + 2xy + y^2$$
$$(x+y)^3 = x^3 + 3x^2y + 3xy^2 + y^3$$
$$(x+y)^4 = x^4 + 4x^3y + 6x^2y^2 + 4xy^3 + y^4$$
$$(x+y)^5 = x^5 + 5x^4y + 10x^3y^2 + 10x^2y^3 + 5xy^4 + y^5.$$

Formula (1) is valid more generally for any elements x and y of a semiring as long as xy = yx.

a. Trinomial expansion
b. Hypergeometric identities
c. Binomial theorem
d. Central binomial coefficient

24. This article will state and prove the _____ for differentiation, and then use it to prove these two formulas.

The _____ for differentiation states that for every natural number n, the derivative of $f(x) = x^n$ is $f'(x) = nx^{n-1}$, that is,

$$(x^n)' = nx^{n-1}.$$

The _____ for integration

$$\int x^n \, dx = \frac{x^{n+1}}{n+1} + C$$

for natural n is then an easy consequence. One just needs to take the derivative of this equality and use the _____ and linearity of differentiation on the right-hand side.

a. Leibniz rule
b. Functional integration
c. Power rule
d. Test for Divergence

Chapter 2. Limits and Derivatives

25. A _____ officer is an officer of high military rank. The term or equivalent is used by nearly every country in the world. _____ can be used as a generic term for all grades of _____ officer, or it can specifically refer to a single rank that is just called _____.
    a. General
    b. 15 theorem
    c. BDDC
    d. BIBO stability

26. In calculus, the _____ is a formula used to find the derivatives of products of functions. It may be stated thus:

$$(f \cdot g)' = f' \cdot g + f \cdot g'$$

or in the Leibniz notation thus:

$$\frac{d}{dx}(u \cdot v) = u \cdot \frac{dv}{dx} + v \cdot \frac{du}{dx}.$$

Discovery of this rule is credited to Gottfried Leibniz, who demonstrated it using differentials. Here is Leibniz's argument: Let u and v be two differentiable functions of x.

   a. Product rule
   b. Differentiation rules
   c. Constant factor rule in differentiation
   d. Quotient Rule

27. In calculus, the _____ is a method of finding the derivative of a function that is the quotient of two other functions for which derivatives exist.

If the function one wishes to differentiate, f(x), can be written as

$$f(x) = \frac{g(x)}{h(x)}$$

and h(x) ≠ 0, then the rule states that the derivative of g(x) / h(x) is equal to:

$$\frac{d}{dx}f(x) = f'(x) = \frac{g'(x)h(x) - g(x)h'(x)}{[h(x)]^2}.$$

Or, more precisely, if all x in some open set containing the number a satisfy h(x) ≠ 0; and g'(a) and h'(a) both exist; then, f'(a) exists as well and:

$$f'(a) = \frac{g'(a)h(a) - g(a)h'(a)}{[h(a)]^2}.$$

The derivative of (4x − 2) / (x² + 1) is:

$$\frac{d}{dx}\left[\frac{(4x-2)}{x^2+1}\right] = \frac{(x^2+1)(4) - (4x-2)(2x)}{(x^2+1)^2}$$
$$= \frac{(4x^2+4) - (8x^2-4x)}{(x^2+1)^2} = \frac{-4x^2+4x+4}{(x^2+1)^2}$$

In the example above, the choices

g(x) = 4x − 2
h(x) = x² + 1

were made. Analogously, the derivative of sin(x) / x² (when x ≠ 0) is:

$$\frac{\cos(x)x^2 - \sin(x)2x}{x^4}$$

Another example is:

$$f(x) = \frac{2x^2}{x^3}$$

whereas g(x) = 2x² and h(x) = x³, and g'(x) = 4x and h'(x) = 3x².

a. Reciprocal Rule
b. Quotient rule
c. Differentiation rules
d. Constant factor rule in differentiation

Chapter 2. Limits and Derivatives

28. In computer science and information science, _____ could also be a method or an algorithm. Again, an example will illustrate: There are systems of counting, as with Roman numerals, and various systems for filing papers, or catalogues, and various library systems, of which the Dewey Decimal _____ is an example. This still fits with the definition of components which are connected together (in this case in order to facilitate the flow of information.)
   a. 15 theorem
   b. BIBO stability
   c. BDDC
   d. System

29. _____ is a method of mathematical proof typically used to establish that a given statement is true of all natural numbers. It is done by proving that the first statement in the infinite sequence of statements is true, and then proving that if any one statement in the infinite sequence of statements is true, then so is the next one.

The method can be extended to prove statements about more general well-founded structures, such as trees; this generalization, known as structural induction, is used in mathematical logic and computer science.

   a. Mathematical induction
   b. BDDC
   c. BIBO stability
   d. 15 theorem

30. Let f be a differentiable function, and let f'(x) be its derivative. The derivative of f'(x) (if it has one) is written f''(x) and is called the _____ of f. Similarly, the derivative of a _____, if it exists, is written f'''(x) and is called the third derivative of f.
   a. Stationary phase approximation
   b. Second derivative
   c. Slant asymptote
   d. Vertical asymptote

31. In mathematics, _____ refers to any of a number of loosely related concepts in different areas of geometry. Intuitively, _____ is the amount by which a geometric object deviates from being flat, or straight in the case of a line, but this is defined in different ways depending on the context. There is a key distinction between extrinsic _____, which is defined for objects embedded in another space (usually a Euclidean space) in a way that relates to the radius of _____ of circles that touch the object, and intrinsic _____, which is defined at each point in a differential manifold.
   a. Lie derivative
   b. Minimal surface
   c. Sphere
   d. Curvature

32. In differential calculus, an inflection point, or _____ (or inflexion) is a point on a curve at which the curvature changes sign. The curve changes from being concave upwards (positive curvature) to concave downwards (negative curvature), or vice versa. If one imagines driving a vehicle along the curve, it is a point at which the steering-wheel is momentarily 'straight', being turned from left to right or vice versa.
    a. Derivative of a constant
    b. Lin-Tsien equation
    c. Logarithmic derivative
    d. Point of inflection

33. In physics, and more specifically kinematics, _____ is the change in velocity over time. Because velocity is a vector, it can change in two ways: a change in magnitude and/or a change in direction. In one dimension, _____ is the rate at which something speeds up or slows down.
    a. ACTRAN
    b. AUSM
    c. ALGOR
    d. Acceleration

34. The _____ is a function in mathematics. The application of this function to a value x is written as exp(x). Equivalently, this can be written in the form e^x, where e is a mathematical constant, the base of the natural logarithm, which equals approximately 2.718281828, and is also known as Euler's number.
    a. Area hyperbolic functions
    b. ACTRAN
    c. Integral part
    d. Exponential function

35. In probability theory and statistics, the _____ is a two-parameter family of continuous probability distributions. It has a scale parameter θ and a shape parameter k. If k is an integer then the distribution represents the sum of k independent exponentially distributed random variables, each of which has a mean of θ (which is equivalent to a rate parameter of $θ^{-1}$).
    a. Nakagami distribution
    b. BDDC
    c. 15 theorem
    d. Gamma distribution

36. The _____ is an important family of continuous probability distributions, applicable in many fields. Each member of the family may be defined by two parameters, location and scale: the mean and variance respectively. The standard _____ is the _____ with a mean of zero and a variance of one.

a. Continuous random variable
b. Moment
c. Normal distribution
d. Correlation

37. In a totally ordered set all elements are mutually comparable, so such a set can have at most one minimal element and at most one maximal element. Then, due to mutual comparability, the minimal element will also be the least element and the maximal element will also be the greatest element. Thus in a totally ordered set we can simply use the terms minimum and _____.

a. Racetrack principle
b. Leibniz rule
c. Nth term
d. Maximum

38. In calculus, the _____ is a formula for the derivative of the composite of two functions.

In intuitive terms, if a variable, y, depends on a second variable, u, which in turn depends on a third variable, x, then the rate of change of y with respect to x can be computed as the rate of change of y with respect to u multiplied by the rate of change of u with respect to x. Schematically,

$$\frac{dy}{dx} = \frac{dy}{du} \cdot \frac{du}{dx}.$$

a. Product rule
b. Reciprocal Rule
c. Differentiation rules
d. Chain rule

39. In mathematics, the _____ of a function y = f(x) is a function that, in some fashion, 'undoes' the effect of f The _____ of f is denoted f^{-1}. The statements y=f(x) and x=f^{-1}(y) are equivalent.

a. Inverse
b. AUSM
c. ACTRAN
d. ALGOR

Chapter 2. Limits and Derivatives

40. In mathematics, if f is a function from A to B then an _____ for f is a function in the opposite direction, from B to A, with the property that a round trip (a composition) from A to B to A (or from B to A to B) returns each element of the initial set to itself. Thus, if an input x into the function f produces an output y, then inputting y into the _____ f^{-1} (read f inverse, not to be confused with exponentiation) produces the output x. Not every function has an inverse; those that do are called invertible.

   a. Augustin Louis Cauchy
   b. Aristotle
   c. Augustin-Jean Fresnel
   d. Inverse function

41. The _____ of an angle is the ratio of the length of the adjacent side to the length of the hypotenuse. In our case

$$\cos A = \frac{\text{adjacent}}{\text{hypotenuse}} = \frac{b}{h}.$$

The tangent of an angle is the ratio of the length of the opposite side to the length of the adjacent side. In our case

$$\tan A = \frac{\text{opposite}}{\text{adjacent}} = \frac{a}{b}.$$

The remaining three functions are best defined using the above three functions.

   a. Sine integral
   b. Cosine
   c. Trigonometric
   d. Trigonometric functions

42. The _____ of an angle is the ratio of the length of the opposite side to the length of the hypotenuse. In our case

$$\sin A = \frac{\text{opposite}}{\text{hypotenuse}} = \frac{a}{h}.$$

Note that this ratio does not depend on size of the particular right triangle chosen, as long as it contains the angle A, since all such triangles are similar.

The cosine of an angle is the ratio of the length of the adjacent side to the length of the hypotenuse.

a. Sine integral
b. Trigonometric
c. Sine
d. Trigonometric functions

43. Trigonometry is a branch of mathematics that deals with triangles, particularly those plane triangles in which one angle has 90 degrees (right triangles.) Trigonometry deals with relationships between the sides and the angles of triangles and with the _____ functions, which describe those relationships.

Trigonometry has applications in both pure mathematics and in applied mathematics, where it is essential in many branches of science and technology.

a. Trigonometric integrals
b. Trigonometric functions
c. Trigonometric
d. Sine

44. In mathematics, the _____ are functions of an angle. They are important in the study of triangles and modeling periodic phenomena, among many other applications. _____ are commonly defined as ratios of two sides of a right triangle containing the angle, and can equivalently be defined as the lengths of various line segments from a unit circle.

a. Trigonometric integrals
b. Trigonometric functions
c. Trigonometric
d. Sine integral

45. In mathematics, in the field of ordinary differential equations, a non trivial solution to an ordinary differential equation

$$F(x, y, y', \ldots, y^{(n-1)}) = y^{(n)} \quad x \in [0, +\infty)$$

is called _____ if it has an infinite number of roots, otherwise it is called non-_____. The differential equation is called _____ if it has an _____ solution.

The differential equation

y" + y = 0

is _____ as sin(x) is a solution.

a. Exponential growth
b. Oscillating
c. Integrating factor
d. Inseparable differential equation

46. In acoustics and telecommunication, a _____ of a wave is a component frequency of the signal that is an integer multiple of the fundamental frequency. For example, if the fundamental frequency is f, the harmonics have frequencies f, 2f, 3f, 4f, etc. The harmonics have the property that they are all periodic at the fundamental frequency, therefore the sum of harmonics is also periodic at that frequency.
   a. BIBO stability
   b. Harmonic
   c. 15 theorem
   d. BDDC

47. In classical mechanics, a _____ is a system which, when displaced from its equilibrium position, experiences a restoring force F proportional to the displacement x according to Hooke's law:

$$F = -kx$$

where k is a positive constant.

If F is the only force acting on the system, the system is called a simple _____, and it undergoes simple harmonic motion: sinusoidal oscillations about the equilibrium point, with a constant amplitude and a constant frequency (which does not depend on the amplitude.)

If a frictional force (damping) proportional to the velocity is also present, the _____ is described as a damped oscillator.

   a. BDDC
   b. BIBO stability
   c. 15 theorem
   d. Harmonic oscillator

Chapter 3. Applications of Derivatives and Dynamical Systems

1. In mathematics, an autonomous system or _____ is a system of ordinary differential equations which does not depend on the independent variable.

Many laws in physics, where the independent variable is usually assumed to be time, are expressed as autonomous systems because it is assumed the laws of nature which hold now are identical to those for any point in the past or future.

Autonomous systems are closely related to dynamical systems.

   a. Annihilator method
   b. Algebraic differential equation
   c. Integro-differential equation
   d. Autonomous differential equation

2. In infinitesimal calculus, a _____ is traditionally an infinitesimally small change in a variable. For example, if x is a variable, then a change in the value of x is often denoted Δx (or δx when this change is considered to be small.) The _____ dx represents such a change, but is infinitely small.
   a. Differential
   b. Dirichlet integral
   c. The Method of Mechanical Theorems
   d. Local maximum

3. A _____ is a mathematical equation for an unknown function of one or several variables that relates the values of the function itself and of its derivatives of various orders. they play a prominent role in engineering, physics, economics and other disciplines.

A simplified real world example of a _____ is modeling the acceleration of a ball falling through the air (considering only gravity and air resistance.)

   a. Structural stability
   b. Caloric polynomial
   c. Phase line
   d. Differential equation

4. In computer science and information science, _____ could also be a method or an algorithm. Again, an example will illustrate: There are systems of counting, as with Roman numerals, and various systems for filing papers, or catalogues, and various library systems, of which the Dewey Decimal _____ is an example. This still fits with the definition of components which are connected together (in this case in order to facilitate the flow of information.)

Chapter 3. Applications of Derivatives and Dynamical Systems

a. BDDC
b. 15 theorem
c. System
d. BIBO stability

5. _____ is used to describe the steepness, incline, gradient, or grade of a straight line. A higher _____ value indicates a steeper incline. The _____ is defined as the ratio of the 'rise' divided by the 'run' between two points on a line, or in other words, the ratio of the altitude change to the horizontal distance between any two points on the line.

a. Slope
b. Y-intercept
c. 15 theorem
d. Sequence

6. In chemistry, _____ is the measure of how much of a given substance there is mixed with another substance. This can apply to any sort of chemical mixture, but most frequently the concept is limited to homogeneous solutions, where it refers to the amount of solute in the solvent.

To concentrate a solution, one must add more solute, or reduce the amount of solvent (for instance, by selective evaporation.)

a. Concentration
b. BDDC
c. BIBO stability
d. 15 theorem

7. The _____ is a polynomial mapping of degree 2, often cited as an archetypal example of how complex, chaotic behaviour can arise from very simple non-linear dynamical equations. The map was popularized in a seminal 1976 paper by the biologist Robert May, in part as a discrete-time demographic model analogous to the logistic equation first created by Pierre François Verhulst. Mathematically, the _____ is written

$$(1) \quad x_{n+1} = rx_n(1 - x_n)$$

where:

x_n is a number between zero and one, and represents the population at year n, and hence x_0 represents the initial population (at year 0)
r is a positive number, and represents a combined rate for reproduction and starvation.

a. BDDC
b. BIBO stability
c. Logistic map
d. 15 theorem

8. In geometry, the _____ (or simply the tangent) to a curve at a given point is the straight line that 'just touches' the curve at that point (in the sense explained more precisely below.) As it passes through the point of tangency, the _____ is 'going in the same direction' as the curve, and in this sense it is the best straight-line approximation to the curve at that point. The same definition applies to space curves and curves in n-dimensional Euclidean space.
   a. North pole
   b. Minimal surface
   c. Tangent line
   d. Lie derivative

9. In mathematics, particularly in dynamical systems, a _____ shows the possible long-term values (equilibria/fixed points or periodic orbits) of a system as a function of a bifurcation parameter in the system. It is usual to represent stable solutions with a solid line and unstable solutions with a dotted line. _____ of the logistic map Animation showing the formation of _____.

An example is the _____ of the logistic map:

$$x_{n+1} = rx_n(1 - x_n).$$

The bifurcation parameter r is shown on the horizontal axis of the plot and the vertical axis shows the possible long-term population values of the logistic function.

   a. BIBO stability
   b. BDDC
   c. 15 theorem
   d. Bifurcation diagram

10. A _____ is a 2D geometric symbolic representation of information according to some visualization technique. Sometimes, the technique uses a 3D visualization which is then projected onto the 2D surface.

_____ has two meanings in common sense.

a. BIBO stability
b. BDDC
c. 15 theorem
d. Diagram

11. _____ is the change in population over time, and can be quantified as the change in the number of individuals in a population using 'per unit time' for measurement. The term _____ can technically refer to any species, but almost always refers to humans, and it is often used informally for the more specific demographic term _____ rate , and is often used to refer specifically to the growth of the population of the world.

Simple models of _____ include the Malthusian Growth Model and the logistic model.

a. 15 theorem
b. BDDC
c. Population growth
d. BIBO stability

12. In mathematics, in the field of ordinary differential equations, a non trivial solution to an ordinary differential equation

$$F(x,y,y', \ldots, y^{(n-1)}) = y^{(n)} \quad x \in [0, +\infty)$$

is called _____ if it has an infinite number of roots, otherwise it is called non-_____. The differential equation is called _____ if it has an _____ solution.

The differential equation

y" + y = 0

is _____ as sin(x) is a solution.

a. Exponential growth
b. Oscillating
c. Integrating factor
d. Inseparable differential equation

Chapter 3. Applications of Derivatives and Dynamical Systems

13. In mathematics, a _____ (or critical number) is a point on the domain of a function where:

    - one dimension: the derivative (or slope of the line when visualized) is equal to zero or a point where the function ceases to be differentiable.
    - in general: there are two distinct concepts: either the derivative (Jacobian) vanishes, or it is not of full rank (or, in either case, the function is not differentiable); these agree in one dimension.

Note that in one dimension, a critical value or critical number x of function f is the domain element at which the derivative is zero or undefined, whereas the associated ordered pair (x, y) is the _____. In higher dimensions a critical value is in the range whereas a _____ is in the domain.

There are two situations in which a point becomes a _____ of a function of one variable. The first of which is that the value of the first derivative is equal to zero.

   a. Multivariable calculus
   b. Total derivative
   c. Differentiation operator
   d. Critical point

14. In a totally ordered set all elements are mutually comparable, so such a set can have at most one minimal element and at most one maximal element. Then, due to mutual comparability, the minimal element will also be the least element and the maximal element will also be the greatest element. Thus in a totally ordered set we can simply use the terms minimum and _____.

   a. Racetrack principle
   b. Leibniz rule
   c. Nth term
   d. Maximum

15. In a totally ordered set all elements are mutually comparable, so such a set can have at most one minimal element and at most one maximal element. Then, due to mutual comparability, the minimal element will also be the least element and the maximal element will also be the greatest element. Thus in a totally ordered set we can simply use the terms _____ and maximum.

   a. Ghosts of departed quantities
   b. Maximum
   c. Nth term
   d. Minimum

16. In mathematics, _____ and minima, known collectively as extrema, are the largest value (maximum) or smallest value (minimum), that a function takes in a point either within a given neighbourhood (local extremum) or on the function domain in its entirety (global extremum.)

Throughout, a point refers to an input (x), while a value refers to an output (y): one distinguishing between the maximum value and the point (or points) at which it occurs.

A real-valued function f defined on the real line is said to have a local maximum point at the point x*, if there exists some ε > 0, such that $f(x^*) \geq f(x)$ when $|x - x^*| < \varepsilon$.

a. Maxima
b. Leibniz formula
c. Racetrack principle
d. Related rates

17. A real-valued function f defined on the real line is said to have a _____ point at the point x>*, if there exists some >ε > 0, such that $f(x^{>*}) \geq f(x)$ when $|x >- x^{>*}| < >\varepsilon$. The value of the function at this point is called maximum of the function.

On a graph of a function, its local maxima will look like the tops of hills.

a. Racetrack principle
b. Local maximum
c. Test for Divergence
d. Standard part function

18. Let f be a differentiable function, and let f'(x) be its derivative. The derivative of f'(x) (if it has one) is written f''(x) and is called the _____ of f. Similarly, the derivative of a _____, if it exists, is written f'''(x) and is called the third derivative of f.

a. Stationary phase approximation
b. Slant asymptote
c. Second derivative
d. Vertical asymptote

19. In calculus, a branch of mathematics, the _____ is a measurement of how a function changes when its input changes. Loosely speaking, a _____ can be thought of as how much a quantity is changing at some given point. For example, the _____ of the position (or distance) of a vehicle with respect to time is the instantaneous velocity (respectively, instantaneous speed) at which the vehicle is traveling.

The process of finding a _____ is called differentiation. The fundamental theorem of calculus states that differentiation is the reverse process to integration.

Chapter 3. Applications of Derivatives and Dynamical Systems

a. Semi-differentiability
b. Bounded function
c. Stationary phase approximation
d. Derivative

20. In mathematics, a _____ is a function for which, intuitively, small changes in the input result in small changes in the output. Otherwise, a function is said to be discontinuous. A _____ with a continuous inverse function is called bicontinuous. An intuitive though imprecise (and inexact) idea of continuity is given by the common statement that a _____ is a function whose graph can be drawn without lifting the chalk from the blackboard.

a. Visual Calculus
b. Binomial series
c. Continuous function
d. Hyperbolic angle

21. In mathematical analysis, the _____ states that for each value between the least upper bound and greatest lower bound of the image of a continuous function there is a corresponding value in its domain mapping to the original. _____

- Version I. The _____ states the following: If the function y = f(x) is continuous on the interval [a, b], and u is a number between f(a) and f(b), then there is a c ∈ [a, b] such that f(c) = u.

- Version II. Suppose that I is an interval [a, b] in the real numbers R and that f : I → R is a continuous function. Then the image set f(I) is also an interval, and either it contains [f(a), f(b)], or it contains [f(b), f(a)]; that is,

    f(I) ⊇ [f(a), f(b)], or f(I) ⊇ [f(b), f(a)].

It is frequently stated in the following equivalent form: Suppose that f : [a, b] → R is continuous and that u is a real number satisfying f(a) < u < f(b) or f(a) > u > f(b).) Then for some c ∈ [a, b], f(c) = u.

This captures an intuitive property of continuous functions: given f continuous on [1, 2], if f(1) = 3 and f(2) = 5 then f must take the value 4 somewhere between 1 and 2.

a. ACTRAN
b. AUSM
c. ALGOR
d. Intermediate Value Theorem

22. The largest and the smallest element of a set are called extreme values, absolute extrema, or extreme records.

For a differentiable function f, if f(x₀) is an _____ for the set of all values f(x), and if x₀ is in the interior of the domain of f, then x₀ is a critical point, by Fermat's theorem.

In the case of a general partial order one should not confuse a least element (smaller than all other) and a minimal element (nothing is smaller.)

   a. Integration by substitution
   b. Extreme Value
   c. Extreme Value Theorem
   d. Infinitesimal

23. In calculus, the _____ states that if a real-valued function f is continuous in the closed and bounded interval [a,b], then f must attain its maximum and minimum value, each at least once. That is, there exist numbers c and d in [a,b] such that:

$$f(c) \geq f(x) \geq f(d) \quad \text{for all } x \in [a,b].$$

A related theorem is the boundedness theorem which states that a continuous function f in the closed interval [a,b] is bounded on that interval. That is, there exist real numbers m and M such that:

$$m \leq f(x) \leq M \quad \text{for all } x \in [a,b].$$

The _____ enriches the boundedness theorem by saying that not only is the function bounded, but it also attains its least upper bound as its maximum and its greatest lower bound as its minimum.

   a. Uniform convergence
   b. Infinitesimal
   c. Integral of secant cubed
   d. Extreme Value Theorem

24. In probability theory and statistics, the _____ (or expectation value or mean and for continuous random variables with a density function it is the probability density-weighted integral of the possible values.

The term '_____' can be misleading.

Chapter 3. Applications of Derivatives and Dynamical Systems

a. Expected value
b. AUSM
c. ACTRAN
d. ALGOR

25. In calculus, the _____ states, roughly, that given a section of a smooth curve, there is at least one point on that section at which the derivative (slope) of the curve is equal (parallel) to the 'average' derivative of the section. It is used to prove theorems that make global conclusions about a function on an interval starting from local hypotheses about derivatives at points of the interval.

This theorem can be understood concretely by applying it to motion: If a car travels one hundred miles in one hour, so its average speed during that time was 100 miles per hour.

a. Periodic function
b. Limits of integration
c. Hyperbolic angle
d. Mean Value Theorem

26. In physics, _____ is defined as the rate of change of position. it is vector physical quantity; both speed and direction are required to define it. In the SI (metric) system, it is measured in meters per second: (m/s) or ms^{-1}.
a. BDDC
b. 15 theorem
c. Velocity
d. BIBO stability

27. The _____, H, also called the unit step function, is a discontinuous function whose value is zero for negative argument and one for positive argument. It seldom matters what value is used for H, since H is mostly used as a distribution. The function is used in the mathematics of control theory and signal processing to represent a signal that switches on at a specified time and stays switched on indefinitely.
a. Heaviside step function
b. Hyperbolic functions
c. Square root function
d. Hyperbolic sine

28. In mathematics, the concept of a '_____' is used to describe the behavior of a function as its argument or input either 'gets close' to some point, or as the argument becomes arbitrarily large; or the behavior of a sequence's elements as their index increases indefinitely. Limits are used in calculus and other branches of mathematical analysis to define derivatives and continuity.

In formulas, _____ is usually abbreviated as lim

 a. BDDC
 b. BIBO stability
 c. 15 theorem
 d. Limit

29. In mathematics, a _____ is an ordered list of objects (or events). Like a set, it contains members (also called elements or terms), and the number of terms (possibly infinite) is called the length of the _____. Unlike a set, order matters, and the exact same elements can appear multiple times at different positions in the _____.
 a. Y-intercept
 b. Slope
 c. 15 theorem
 d. Sequence

30. In calculus and other branches of mathematical analysis, an _____ is an algebraic expression obtained in the context of limits. Limits involving algebraic operations are often performed by replacing subexpressions by their limits; if the expression obtained after this substitution does not give enough information to determine the original limit, it is known as an _____. The indeterminate forms include 0^0, $0/0$, 1^∞, $\infty - \infty$, ∞/∞, $0\times\infty$, and ∞^0.
 a. ALGOR
 b. AUSM
 c. ACTRAN
 d. Indeterminate form

31. The _____ is a function in mathematics. The application of this function to a value x is written as exp(x). Equivalently, this can be written in the form e^x, where e is a mathematical constant, the base of the natural logarithm, which equals approximately 2.718281828, and is also known as Euler's number.
 a. Exponential function
 b. ACTRAN
 c. Integral part
 d. Area hyperbolic functions

32. The _____, formerly known as the hyperbolic logarithm, is the logarithm to the base e, where e is an irrational constant approximately equal to 2.718281828. It is also sometimes referred to as the Napierian logarithm, although the original meaning of this term is slightly different. In simple terms, the _____ of a number x is the power to which e would have to be raised to equal x -- for example the natural log of e itself is 1 because e^1 = e, while the _____ of 1 would be 0, since e^0 = 1.

a. BDDC
b. BIBO stability
c. 15 theorem
d. Natural logarithm

33. A _____ of a curve is a line that (locally) intersects two points on the curve. The word secant comes from the Latin secare, for to cut.

It can be used to approximate the tangent to a curve, at some point P. If the secant to a curve is defined by two points, P and Q, with P fixed and Q variable, as Q approaches P along the curve, the direction of the secant approaches that of the tangent at P, assuming there is just one.

a. Kappa curve
b. Curve
c. Witch of Agnesi
d. Secant line

34. In the mathematical subfield of numerical analysis, _____ is a method of constructing new data points within the range of a discrete set of known data points.

In engineering and science one often has a number of data points, as obtained by sampling or experimentation, and tries to construct a function which closely fits those data points. This is called curve fitting or regression analysis.

a. ALGOR
b. AUSM
c. ACTRAN
d. Interpolation

35. A _____, in mathematics, is a polynomial function of the form $f(x) = ax^2 + bx + c$, where $a \neq 0$. The graph of a _____ is a parabola whose major axis is parallel to the y-axis.

The expression $ax^2 + bx + c$ in the definition of a _____ is a polynomial of degree 2 or a 2nd degree polynomial, because the highest exponent of x is 2.

a. Resultant
b. Quadratic function
c. Leading coefficient
d. Discriminant

36. In mathematics, the _____ of a non-negative integer n, denoted by n!, is the product of all positive integers less than or equal to n. For example,

$$5! = 1 \times 2 \times 3 \times 4 \times 5 = 120$$

and

$$6! = 1 \times 2 \times 3 \times 4 \times 5 \times 6 = 720.$$

The notation n! was introduced by Christian Kramp in 1808.

The _____ function is formally defined by

$$n! = \prod_{k=1}^{n} k \qquad \forall n \in \mathbb{N}$$

or recursively defined by

$$n! = \begin{cases} n \leq 1 & 1 \\ n > 1 & n(n-1)! \end{cases} \qquad \forall n \in \mathbb{N}.$$

Both of the above definitions incorporate the instance

$$0! = 1$$

as an instance of the fact that the product of no numbers at all is 1.

a. Constraint counting
b. 15 theorem
c. BDDC
d. Factorial

Chapter 3. Applications of Derivatives and Dynamical Systems 43

37. In calculus, _____ gives a sequence of approximations of a differentiable function around a given point by polynomials (the Taylor polynomials of that function) whose coefficients depend only on the derivatives of the function at that point. The theorem also gives precise estimates on the size of the error in the approximation. The theorem is named after the mathematician Brook Taylor, who stated it in 1712, though the result was first discovered 41 years earlier in 1671 by James Gregory.
    a. Fresnel integrals
    b. Taylor's theorem
    c. Local minimum
    d. Related rates

38. Cantor defined two kinds of _____ numbers, the ordinal numbers and the cardinal numbers. Ordinal numbers may be identified with well-ordered sets, or counting carried on to any stopping point, including points after an _____ number have already been counted. Generalizing finite and the ordinary _____ sequences which are maps from the positive integers leads to mappings from ordinal numbers, and transfinite sequences.
    a. ACTRAN
    b. ALGOR
    c. AUSM
    d. Infinite

39. The terms of the series are often produced according to a certain rule, such as by a formula, by an algorithm, by a sequence of measurements, or even by a random number generator. As there are an infinite number of terms, this notion is often called an _____. Unlike finite summations, series need tools from mathematical analysis to be fully understood and manipulated.
    a. Infinite series
    b. Extreme Value Theorem
    c. Integration by substitution
    d. Extreme value

40. In geometry, _____ is the division of something into two equal or congruent parts, usually by a line, which is then called a bisector. The most often considered types of bisectors are segment bisectors and angle bisectors. _____ of a line segment using a compass and ruler _____ of an angle using a compass and ruler Line DE bisects line AB at D, line EF is a perpendicular bisector of segment AD at C and the interior bisector of right angle AED

A line segment bisector passes through the midpoint of the segment.

a. 15 theorem
b. BIBO stability
c. BDDC
d. Bisection

Chapter 4. Differential Equations, Integrals, and Their Applications 45

1. In calculus, an _____, primitive or indefinite integral of a function f is a function F whose derivative is equal to f, i.e., F >' = f. The process of solving for antiderivatives is antidifferentiation (or indefinite integration.) Antiderivatives are related to definite integrals through the fundamental theorem of calculus: the definite integral of a function over an interval is equal to the difference between the values of an _____ evaluated at the endpoints of the interval.
    a. Integrand
    b. Order of integration
    c. Antiderivative
    d. Indefinite integral

2. In calculus, an antiderivative, primitive or _____ of a function f is a function F whose derivative is equal to f, i.e., F ' = f. The process of solving for antiderivatives is antidifferentiation (or indefinite integration.) Antiderivatives are related to definite integrals through the fundamental theorem of calculus: the definite integral of a function over an interval is equal to the difference between the values of an antiderivative evaluated at the endpoints of the interval.
    a. Arc length
    b. Indefinite integral
    c. Integration by parts operator
    d. Integral test for convergence

3. Integration is an important concept in mathematics, specifically in the field of calculus and, more broadly, mathematical analysis. Given a function f of a real variable x and an interval [a, b] of the real line, the _____

$$\int_a^b f(x)\,dx,$$

is defined informally to be the net signed area of the region in the xy-plane bounded by the graph of f, the x-axis, and the vertical lines x = a and x = b.

The term '_____' may also refer to the notion of antiderivative, a function F whose derivative is the given function f.

    a. Integrand
    b. Integral test for convergence
    c. Indefinite integral
    d. Integral

4. If a function has an integral, it is said to be integrable. The function for which the integral is calculated is called the _____. The region over which a function is being integrated is called the domain of integration.

a. Order of integration
b. Integral test for convergence
c. Integration by parts
d. Integrand

5. _____ is a type of motion in which the velocity of an object changes equal amounts in equal time periods. An example of an object having _____ would be a ball rolling down a ramp. The object picks up velocity as it goes down the ramp with equal changes in time.
   a. AUSM
   b. ALGOR
   c. ACTRAN
   d. Uniform Acceleration

6. In calculus, the indefinite integral of a given function (i.e. the set of all antiderivatives of the function) is always written with a constant, the _____. This constant expresses an ambiguity inherent in the construction of antiderivatives. If a function f(x) is defined on an interval and F(x) is an antiderivative of f(x), then the set of all antiderivatives of f(x) is given by the functions F(x) + C, where C is an arbitrary constant.
   a. Disk integration
   b. Sum rule in integration
   c. Constant of integration
   d. Nonelementary integral

7. In calculus, a branch of mathematics, the _____ is a measurement of how a function changes when its input changes. Loosely speaking, a _____ can be thought of as how much a quantity is changing at some given point. For example, the _____ of the position (or distance) of a vehicle with respect to time is the instantaneous velocity (respectively, instantaneous speed) at which the vehicle is traveling.

The process of finding a _____ is called differentiation. The fundamental theorem of calculus states that differentiation is the reverse process to integration.

   a. Bounded function
   b. Stationary phase approximation
   c. Derivative
   d. Semi-differentiability

Chapter 4. Differential Equations, Integrals, and Their Applications

8. In integral calculus we would want to write a fractional algebraic expression as the sum of its _____ in order to take the integral of each simple fraction separately. Once the original denominator, D_0, has been factored we set up a fraction for each factor in the denominator. We may use a subscripted D to represent the denominator of the respective _____ which are the factors in D_0.
   a. Multinomial theorem
   b. Closed-form expression
   c. Left inverse
   d. Partial fractions

9. In calculus, the _____ is a formula used to find the derivatives of products of functions. It may be stated thus:

$$(f \cdot g)' = f' \cdot g + f \cdot g'$$

or in the Leibniz notation thus:

$$\frac{d}{dx}(u \cdot v) = u \cdot \frac{dv}{dx} + v \cdot \frac{du}{dx}.$$

Discovery of this rule is credited to Gottfried Leibniz, who demonstrated it using differentials. Here is Leibniz's argument: Let u and v be two differentiable functions of x.

   a. Constant factor rule in differentiation
   b. Quotient Rule
   c. Differentiation rules
   d. Product rule

10. In infinitesimal calculus, a _____ is traditionally an infinitesimally small change in a variable. For example, if x is a variable, then a change in the value of x is often denoted Δx (or δx when this change is considered to be small.) The _____ dx represents such a change, but is infinitely small.
    a. Dirichlet integral
    b. Local maximum
    c. Differential
    d. The Method of Mechanical Theorems

11. A _____ is a mathematical equation for an unknown function of one or several variables that relates the values of the function itself and of its derivatives of various orders. they play a prominent role in engineering, physics, economics and other disciplines.

Chapter 4. Differential Equations, Integrals, and Their Applications

A simplified real world example of a _____ is modeling the acceleration of a ball falling through the air (considering only gravity and air resistance.)

a. Differential equation
b. Structural stability
c. Caloric polynomial
d. Phase line

12. In physics, and more specifically kinematics, _____ is the change in velocity over time. Because velocity is a vector, it can change in two ways: a change in magnitude and/or a change in direction. In one dimension, _____ is the rate at which something speeds up or slows down.
   a. Acceleration
   b. ACTRAN
   c. AUSM
   d. ALGOR

13. The _____ is a function in mathematics. The application of this function to a value x is written as exp(x). Equivalently, this can be written in the form e^x, where e is a mathematical constant, the base of the natural logarithm, which equals approximately 2.718281828, and is also known as Euler's number.
   a. Area hyperbolic functions
   b. ACTRAN
   c. Integral part
   d. Exponential function

14. The _____, formerly known as the hyperbolic logarithm, is the logarithm to the base e, where e is an irrational constant approximately equal to 2.718281828. It is also sometimes referred to as the Napierian logarithm, although the original meaning of this term is slightly different. In simple terms, the _____ of a number x is the power to which e would have to be raised to equal x -- for example the natural log of e itself is 1 because e^1 = e, while the _____ of 1 would be 0, since e^0 = 1.
   a. BIBO stability
   b. 15 theorem
   c. BDDC
   d. Natural logarithm

15. In a totally ordered set all elements are mutually comparable, so such a set can have at most one minimal element and at most one maximal element. Then, due to mutual comparability, the minimal element will also be the least element and the maximal element will also be the greatest element. Thus in a totally ordered set we can simply use the terms minimum and _____.

   a. Leibniz rule
   b. Nth term
   c. Racetrack principle
   d. Maximum

16. In calculus, the _____ is a formula for the derivative of the composite of two functions.

In intuitive terms, if a variable, y, depends on a second variable, u, which in turn depends on a third variable, x, then the rate of change of y with respect to x can be computed as the rate of change of y with respect to u multiplied by the rate of change of u with respect to x. Schematically,

$$\frac{dy}{dx} = \frac{dy}{du} \cdot \frac{du}{dx}.$$

   a. Differentiation rules
   b. Reciprocal Rule
   c. Product rule
   d. Chain rule

17. The _____ of an angle is the ratio of the length of the adjacent side to the length of the hypotenuse. In our case

$$\cos A = \frac{\text{adjacent}}{\text{hypotenuse}} = \frac{b}{h}.$$

The tangent of an angle is the ratio of the length of the opposite side to the length of the adjacent side. In our case

$$\tan A = \frac{\text{opposite}}{\text{adjacent}} = \frac{a}{b}.$$

The remaining three functions are best defined using the above three functions.

a. Trigonometric
b. Sine integral
c. Trigonometric functions
d. Cosine

18. The _____ of an angle is the ratio of the length of the opposite side to the length of the hypotenuse. In our case

$$\sin A = \frac{\text{opposite}}{\text{hypotenuse}} = \frac{a}{h}.$$

Note that this ratio does not depend on size of the particular right triangle chosen, as long as it contains the angle A, since all such triangles are similar.

The cosine of an angle is the ratio of the length of the adjacent side to the length of the hypotenuse.

a. Sine integral
b. Trigonometric
c. Trigonometric functions
d. Sine

19. In calculus, _____ is a tool for finding antiderivatives and integrals. Using the fundamental theorem of calculus often requires finding an antiderivative. For this and other reasons, _____ is a relatively important tool for mathematicians.
a. Extreme value
b. Integral of secant cubed
c. Integration by substitution
d. Odd function

20. In mathematics, a function on the real numbers is called a _____ (or staircase function) if it can be written as a finite linear combination of indicator functions of intervals. Informally speaking, a _____ is a piecewise constant function having only finitely many pieces.
a. Step function
b. Square root function
c. Multiplicative inverse
d. Hyperbolic sine

Chapter 4. Differential Equations, Integrals, and Their Applications

21. _____ is the addition of a set of numbers; the result is their sum or total. An interim or present total of a _____ process is termed the running total. The 'numbers' to be summed may be natural numbers, complex numbers, matrices, or still more complicated objects.

    a. 15 theorem
    b. BDDC
    c. BIBO stability
    d. Summation

22. In mathematics, a _____ is a method for approximating the total area underneath a curve on a graph, otherwise known as an integral. It may also be used to define the integration operation.

Consider a function $f: D \to \mathbf{R}$, where D is a subset of the real numbers $\mathbf{R}$, and let $I = [a, b]$ be a closed interval contained in D. A finite set of points $\{x_0, x_1, x_2, ... x_n\}$ such that $a = x_0 < x_1 < x_2 ... < x_n = b$ creates a partition

$$P = \{[x_0, x_1), [x_1, x_2), ... [x_{n-1}, x_n]\}$$

of I.

    a. Solid of revolution
    b. Riemann sum
    c. Risch algorithm
    d. Signed measure

23. In mathematics, the concept of a '_____' is used to describe the behavior of a function as its argument or input either 'gets close' to some point, or as the argument becomes arbitrarily large; or the behavior of a sequence's elements as their index increases indefinitely. Limits are used in calculus and other branches of mathematical analysis to define derivatives and continuity.

In formulas, _____ is usually abbreviated as lim

    a. BIBO stability
    b. 15 theorem
    c. BDDC
    d. Limit

24. In calculus and mathematical analysis the _____ of the integral

$$\int_a^b f(x)\,dx$$

of a Riemann integrable function f defined on a closed and bounded interval [a, b] are the real numbers a and b. _____ can also be defined for improper integrals, with the _____ of both

$$\lim_{z \to a+} \int_z^b f(x)\,dx$$

and

$$\lim_{z \to b-} \int_a^z f(x)\,dx$$

again being a and b. For an improper integral

$$\int_a^\infty f(x)\,dx$$

or

$$\int_{-\infty}^b f(x)\,dx$$

the _____ are a and ∞, or −∞ and b, respectively.

   a. Test for Divergence
   b. Differential
   c. Maxima
   d. Limits of integration

25. In the branch of mathematics known as real analysis, the _____, created by Bernhard Riemann, was the first rigorous definition of the integral of a function on an interval. While the _____ is unsuitable for many theoretical purposes, it is one of the easiest integrals to define. Some of these technical deficiencies can be remedied by the Riemann-Stieltjes integral, and most of them disappear in the Lebesgue integral.

a. Lebesgue integration
b. Skorokhod integral
c. Regulated integral
d. Riemann integral

26. The _____ specifies the relationship between the two central operations of calculus, differentiation and integration.

The first part of the theorem, sometimes called the first _____, shows that an indefinite integration can be reversed by a differentiation.

The second part, sometimes called the second _____, allows one to compute the definite integral of a function by using any one of its infinitely many antiderivatives.

a. Periodic function
b. Limits of integration
c. Leibniz formula
d. Fundamental Theorem of Calculus

27. _____ is any physical or virtual entity that is owned by an individual or jointly by a group of individuals. An owner of _____ has the right to consume, sell, rent, mortgage, transfer and exchange his or her _____. Important widely-recognized types of _____ include real _____, personal _____ (other physical possessions), and intellectual _____ (rights over artistic creations, inventions, etc.), although the latter is not always as widely recognized or enforced.

a. BIBO stability
b. BDDC
c. Property
d. 15 theorem

28. In mathematics, a (topological) _____ is defined as follows: let I be an interval of real numbers (i.e. a non-empty connected subset of $\mathbb{R}$); then a _____ γ is a continuous mapping $\gamma : I \to X$, where X is a topological space. The _____ γ is said to be simple if it is injective, i.e. if for all x, y in I, we have $\gamma(x) = \gamma(y) \implies x = y$. If I is a closed bounded interval $[a, b]$, we also allow the possibility $\gamma(a) = \gamma(b)$ (this convention makes it possible to talk about closed simple _____.)

a. Curve
b. Tractrix
c. Prolate cycloid
d. Closed curve

Chapter 4. Differential Equations, Integrals, and Their Applications

29. The _____ of a material is defined as its mass per unit volume. The symbol of _____ is ρ '>rho.)

Mathematically:

$$d = \frac{m}{V}$$

where:

    d is the _____,
    m is the mass,
    V is the volume.

a. Density
b. BDDC
c. BIBO stability
d. 15 theorem

30. In calculus, an _____ is the limit of a definite integral as an endpoint of the interval of integration approaches either a specified real number or ∞ or −∞ or, in some cases, as both endpoints approach limits.

Specifically, an _____ is a limit of the form

$$\lim_{b \to \infty} \int_a^b f(x)\,dx, \qquad \lim_{a \to -\infty} \int_a^b f(x)\,dx,$$

or of the form

$$\lim_{c \to b^-} \int_a^c f(x)\,dx, \qquad \lim_{c \to a^+} \int_c^b f(x)\,dx,$$

in which one takes a limit in one or the other (or sometimes both) endpoints. Improper integrals may also occur at an interior point of the domain of integration, or at multiple such points.

a. AUSM
b. Improper integral
c. ACTRAN
d. ALGOR

31. Cantor defined two kinds of _____ numbers, the ordinal numbers and the cardinal numbers. Ordinal numbers may be identified with well-ordered sets, or counting carried on to any stopping point, including points after an _____ number have already been counted. Generalizing finite and the ordinary _____ sequences which are maps from the positive integers leads to mappings from ordinal numbers, and transfinite sequences.
   a. ALGOR
   b. AUSM
   c. ACTRAN
   d. Infinite

32. In vector calculus, the _____ is an operator that measures the magnitude of a vector field's source or sink at a given point; the _____ of a vector field is a (signed) scalar. For example, consider air as it is heated or cooled. The relevant vector field for this example is the velocity of the moving air at a point.
   a. Green's theorem
   b. Triple product
   c. Gradient theorem
   d. Divergence

33. In mathematics, the _____, sometimes called the direct _____ is a criterion for convergence or divergence of a series whose terms are real or complex numbers. The test determines convergence by comparing the terms of the series in question with those of a series whose convergence properties are known.

The _____ states that if the series

$$\sum_{n=1}^{\infty} b_n$$

is an absolutely convergent series and

$$|a_n| \leq |b_n|$$

for sufficiently large n, then the series

$$\sum_{n=1}^{\infty} a_n$$

converges absolutely.

a. Conditionally convergent
b. Ratio test
c. Telescoping series
d. Comparison test

34. In acoustics and telecommunication, a _____ of a wave is a component frequency of the signal that is an integer multiple of the fundamental frequency. For example, if the fundamental frequency is f, the harmonics have frequencies f, 2f, 3f, 4f, etc. The harmonics have the property that they are all periodic at the fundamental frequency, therefore the sum of harmonics is also periodic at that frequency.

a. BDDC
b. BIBO stability
c. 15 theorem
d. Harmonic

35. In mathematics, the _____ is the infinite series

$$\sum_{k=1}^{\infty} \frac{1}{k} = 1 + \frac{1}{2} + \frac{1}{3} + \frac{1}{4} + \cdots.$$

Its name derives from the concept of overtones, or harmonics, in music: the wavelengths of the overtones of a vibrating string are 1/2, 1/3, 1/4, etc., of the string's fundamental wavelength. Every term of the series after the first is the harmonic mean of the neighboring terms; the term harmonic mean likewise derives from music.

The _____ diverges to infinity, albeit rather slowly (the first 10^{43} terms sum to less than 100 .)

a. BDDC
b. Harmonic series
c. 15 theorem
d. BIBO stability

36. The terms of the series are often produced according to a certain rule, such as by a formula, by an algorithm, by a sequence of measurements, or even by a random number generator. As there are an infinite number of terms, this notion is often called an _____. Unlike finite summations, series need tools from mathematical analysis to be fully understood and manipulated.

Chapter 4. Differential Equations, Integrals, and Their Applications

a. Extreme value
b. Extreme Value Theorem
c. Integration by substitution
d. Infinite series

37. In numerical analysis, a branch of applied mathematics, the _____ is a one-step method for solving the differential equation

$$y'(t) = f(t, y(t)), \quad y(t_0) = y_0$$

numerically, and is given by the formula

$$y_{n+1} = y_n + hf\left(t_n + \frac{h}{2}, y_n + \frac{h}{2}f(t_n, y_n)\right), \quad (1)$$

for $n = 0, 1, 2, \ldots$ Here, h is the step size -- a small positive number, $t_n = t_0 + nh$, and y_n is the computed approximate value of $y(t_n)$.

The name of the method comes from the fact that in the formula above the function f is evaluated at $t = t_n + h/2$, which is the midpoint between t_n at which the value of y(t) is known and t_{n+1} at which the value of y(t) needs to be found.

The error at each step of the _____ is of order $O(h^3)$. Thus, while more computationally intensive than Euler's method, the _____ generally gives more accurate results.

The method is an example of a class of higher-order methods known as Runge-Kutta methods.

a. Shooting method
b. Midpoint method
c. Discontinuous Galerkin methods
d. Semi-implicit Euler method

38. In mathematics, the Runge - Kutta method is a technique for the approximate numerical solution of a stochastic differential equation. It is a generalization of the _____ for ordinary differential equations to stochastic differential equations.

Consider the Itô diffusion X satisfying the following Itô stochastic differential equation

$$dX_t = a(X_t)\,dt + b(X_t)\,dW_t,$$

with initial condition $X_0 = x_0$, where W_t stands for the Wiener process, and suppose that we wish to solve this SDE on some interval of time [0, T].

- a. Spectral element method
- b. Roe approximate Riemann solver
- c. Parallel mesh generation
- d. Runge-Kutta method

Chapter 5. Analysis of Autonomous Differential Equations

1. In mathematics, an autonomous system or _____ is a system of ordinary differential equations which does not depend on the independent variable.

Many laws in physics, where the independent variable is usually assumed to be time, are expressed as autonomous systems because it is assumed the laws of nature which hold now are identical to those for any point in the past or future.

Autonomous systems are closely related to dynamical systems.

   a. Autonomous differential equation
   b. Algebraic differential equation
   c. Integro-differential equation
   d. Annihilator method

2. In infinitesimal calculus, a _____ is traditionally an infinitesimally small change in a variable. For example, if x is a variable, then a change in the value of x is often denoted Δx (or δx when this change is considered to be small.) The _____ dx represents such a change, but is infinitely small.
   a. The Method of Mechanical Theorems
   b. Dirichlet integral
   c. Local maximum
   d. Differential

3. A _____ is a mathematical equation for an unknown function of one or several variables that relates the values of the function itself and of its derivatives of various orders. they play a prominent role in engineering, physics, economics and other disciplines.

A simplified real world example of a _____ is modeling the acceleration of a ball falling through the air (considering only gravity and air resistance.)

   a. Phase line
   b. Differential equation
   c. Caloric polynomial
   d. Structural stability

4. _____ is the change in population over time, and can be quantified as the change in the number of individuals in a population using 'per unit time' for measurement. The term _____ can technically refer to any species, but almost always refers to humans, and it is often used informally for the more specific demographic term _____ rate , and is often used to refer specifically to the growth of the population of the world.

Simple models of _____ include the Malthusian Growth Model and the logistic model.

a. Population growth
b. BDDC
c. BIBO stability
d. IS theorem

5. In mathematics, in the field of ordinary differential equations, a non trivial solution to an ordinary differential equation

$$F(x, y, y', \ldots, y^{(n-1)}) = y^{(n)} \quad x \in [0, +\infty)$$

is called _____ if it has an infinite number of roots, otherwise it is called non-_____. The differential equation is called _____ if it has an _____ solution.

The differential equation

y" + y = 0

is _____ as sin(x) is a solution.

a. Inseparable differential equation
b. Exponential growth
c. Oscillating
d. Integrating factor

6. In mathematical analysis, the _____ states that for each value between the least upper bound and greatest lower bound of the image of a continuous function there is a corresponding value in its domain mapping to the original. _____

- Version I. The _____ states the following: If the function y = f(x) is continuous on the interval [a, b], and u is a number between f(a) and f(b), then there is a c ∈ [a, b] such that f(c) = u.

- Version II. Suppose that I is an interval [a, b] in the real numbers R and that f : I → R is a continuous function. Then the image set f(I) is also an interval, and either it contains [f(a), f(b)], or it contains [f(b), f(a)]; that is,

    f(I) ⊇ [f(a), f(b)], or f(I) ⊇ [f(b), f(a)].

It is frequently stated in the following equivalent form: Suppose that f : [a, b] → R is continuous and that u is a real number satisfying f(a) < u < f(b) or f(a) > u > f(b.) Then for some c ∈ [a, b], f(c) = u.

This captures an intuitive property of continuous functions: given f continuous on [1, 2], if f(1) = 3 and f(2) = 5 then f must take the value 4 somewhere between 1 and 2.

Chapter 5. Analysis of Autonomous Differential Equations

a. ALGOR
b. ACTRAN
c. AUSM
d. Intermediate Value Theorem

7. A _____ is a 2D geometric symbolic representation of information according to some visualization technique. Sometimes, the technique uses a 3D visualization which is then projected onto the 2D surface.

_____ has two meanings in common sense.

a. BIBO stability
b. 15 theorem
c. BDDC
d. Diagram

8. In mathematics, particularly in dynamical systems, a _____ shows the possible long-term values (equilibria/fixed points or periodic orbits) of a system as a function of a bifurcation parameter in the system. It is usual to represent stable solutions with a solid line and unstable solutions with a dotted line. _____ of the logistic map Animation showing the formation of _____.

An example is the _____ of the logistic map:

$$x_{n+1} = rx_n(1 - x_n).$$

The bifurcation parameter r is shown on the horizontal axis of the plot and the vertical axis shows the possible long-term population values of the logistic function.

a. BIBO stability
b. 15 theorem
c. BDDC
d. Bifurcation diagram

9. In bifurcation theory, a field within mathematics, a _____ is a particular type of local bifurcation. Pitchfork bifurcations, like Hopf bifurcations have two types - supercritical or subcritical.

In flows, that is, continuous dynamical systems described by ODEs, pitchfork bifurcations occur generically in systems with symmetry.

a. Saddle-node bifurcation
b. Catastrophe theory
c. Hopf bifurcation
d. Pitchfork Bifurcation

10. In the mathematical area of bifurcation theory a _____ or tangential bifurcation is a local bifurcation in which two fixed points (or equilibria) of a dynamical system collide and annihilate each other. The term '_____' is most often used in reference to continuous dynamical systems. In discrete dynamical systems, the same bifurcation is often instead called a fold bifurcation.
a. Catastrophe theory
b. Hopf bifurcation
c. Pitchfork bifurcation
d. Saddle-node Bifurcation

11. In mathematics, _____ is any of several methods for solving ordinary and partial differential equations, in which algebra allows one to rewrite an equation so that each of two variables occurs on a different side of the equation.

Suppose a differential equation can be written in the form

$$\frac{d}{dx}f(x) = g(x)h(f(x)), \qquad (1)$$

which we can write more simply by letting y = f(x):

$$\frac{dy}{dx} = g(x)h(y).$$

As long as h(y) ≠ 0, we can rearrange terms to obtain:

$$\frac{dy}{h(y)} = g(x)dx,$$

so that the two variables x and y have been separated.

Some who dislike Leibniz's notation may prefer to write this as

$$\frac{1}{h(y)}\frac{dy}{dx} = g(x),$$

Chapter 5. Analysis of Autonomous Differential Equations   63

but that fails to make it quite as obvious why this is called '_____'.

a. Separation of variables
b. Power series method
c. Damping ratio
d. Sturm separation theorem

12. In integral calculus we would want to write a fractional algebraic expression as the sum of its _____ in order to take the integral of each simple fraction separately. Once the original denominator, D_0, has been factored we set up a fraction for each factor in the denominator. We may use a subscripted D to represent the denominator of the respective _____ which are the factors in D_0.

a. Multinomial theorem
b. Left inverse
c. Closed-form expression
d. Partial fractions

13. The _____ are a pair of first order, non-linear, differential equations frequently used to describe the dynamics of biological systems in which two species interact, one a predator and one its prey. They were proposed independently by Alfred J. Lotka in 1925 and Vito Volterra in 1926.

>

>

where

- y is the number of some predator;
- x is the number of its prey;
- dy/dt and dx/dt represents the growth of the two populations against time;
- t represents the time; and
- >α, >β, >γ and >δ are parameters representing the interaction of the two species.

Chapter 5. Analysis of Autonomous Differential Equations

When multiplied out, the equations take a form useful for physical interpretation. Their origin should be considered from a more general framework,

$$\frac{dx}{dt} = $$
$$\frac{dy}{dt} = $$

where both functions represent per capita growth rates of the prey and predator, respectively.

a. Lotka-Volterra equations
b. BDDC
c. 15 theorem
d. BIBO stability

14. In computer science and information science, _____ could also be a method or an algorithm. Again, an example will illustrate: There are systems of counting, as with Roman numerals, and various systems for filing papers, or catalogues, and various library systems, of which the Dewey Decimal _____ is an example. This still fits with the definition of components which are connected together (in this case in order to facilitate the flow of information.)

a. System
b. 15 theorem
c. BIBO stability
d. BDDC

15. The _____ of a biological species in an environment is the population size of the species that the environment can sustain in the long term, given the food, habitat, water and other necessities available in the environment. For the human population, more complex variables such as sanitation and medical care are sometimes considered as part of the necessary infrastructure.

As population density increases, birth rate often increases and death rate typically decreases.

a. BIBO stability
b. BDDC
c. 15 theorem
d. Carrying capacity

16. In acoustics and telecommunication, a _____ of a wave is a component frequency of the signal that is an integer multiple of the fundamental frequency. For example, if the fundamental frequency is f, the harmonics have frequencies f, 2f, 3f, 4f, etc. The harmonics have the property that they are all periodic at the fundamental frequency, therefore the sum of harmonics is also periodic at that frequency.
   a. BIBO stability
   b. Harmonic
   c. 15 theorem
   d. BDDC

17. In classical mechanics, a _____ is a system which, when displaced from its equilibrium position, experiences a restoring force F proportional to the displacement x according to Hooke's law:

$$F = -kx$$

where k is a positive constant.

If F is the only force acting on the system, the system is called a simple _____, and it undergoes simple harmonic motion: sinusoidal oscillations about the equilibrium point, with a constant amplitude and a constant frequency (which does not depend on the amplitude.)

If a frictional force (damping) proportional to the velocity is also present, the _____ is described as a damped oscillator.

   a. 15 theorem
   b. BDDC
   c. BIBO stability
   d. Harmonic oscillator

18. Nullclines, sometimes called zero-growth isoclines (which were developed by MIT mathematicians in early 20th century), are encountered in two-dimensional systems of differential equations

   x' = F(x,y)
   y' = G(x,y.)

They are curves along which the vector field is either completely horizontal or vertical. A _____ is a boundary between regions where x' or y' switch signs. Nullclines can be found by setting either x' = 0 or y' = 0.

Chapter 5. Analysis of Autonomous Differential Equations

a. Homogeneous differential equation
b. Delay differential equation
c. Riemann-Hilbert correspondence
d. Nullcline

19. A _____ is a visual display of certain characteristics of certain kinds of differential equations.

Phase planes are useful in visualizing the behavior of physical systems; in particular, of oscillatory systems such as predator-prey models These models can 'spiral in' towards zero, 'spiral out' towards infinity, or reach neutrally stable situations called centres where the path traced out can be either circular, elliptical, or ovoid, or some variant thereof.

a. Phase plane
b. Node
c. Spectral theory of ordinary differential equations
d. Boundary value problem

20. A _____ is the path a moving object follows through space. The object might be a projectile or a satellite, for example. It thus includes the meaning of orbit - the path of a planet, an asteroid or a comet as it travels around a central mass.
a. BDDC
b. 15 theorem
c. Trajectory
d. BIBO stability

Chapter 6. Probability Theory and Descriptive Statistics

1. _____ is a way of expressing knowledge or belief that an event will occur or has occurred. In mathematics the concept has been given an exact meaning in _____ theory, that is used extensively in such areas of study as mathematics, statistics, finance, gambling, science, and philosophy to draw conclusions about the likelihood of potential events and the underlying mechanics of complex systems.

The word _____ does not have a consistent direct definition.

  a. Linear regression
  b. Discrete probability distributions
  c. Normal distribution
  d. Probability

2. _____ is the change in population over time, and can be quantified as the change in the number of individuals in a population using 'per unit time' for measurement. The term _____ can technically refer to any species, but almost always refers to humans, and it is often used informally for the more specific demographic term _____ rate , and is often used to refer specifically to the growth of the population of the world.

Simple models of _____ include the Malthusian Growth Model and the logistic model.

  a. Population growth
  b. BIBO stability
  c. 15 theorem
  d. BDDC

3. In computer science and information science, _____ could also be a method or an algorithm. Again, an example will illustrate: There are systems of counting, as with Roman numerals, and various systems for filing papers, or catalogues, and various library systems, of which the Dewey Decimal _____ is an example. This still fits with the definition of components which are connected together (in this case in order to facilitate the flow of information.)

  a. 15 theorem
  b. BIBO stability
  c. BDDC
  d. System

4. In a totally ordered set all elements are mutually comparable, so such a set can have at most one minimal element and at most one maximal element. Then, due to mutual comparability, the minimal element will also be the least element and the maximal element will also be the greatest element. Thus in a totally ordered set we can simply use the terms minimum and _____.

a. Racetrack principle
b. Maximum
c. Nth term
d. Leibniz rule

5. A _____ is a 2D geometric symbolic representation of information according to some visualization technique. Sometimes, the technique uses a 3D visualization which is then projected onto the 2D surface.

_____ has two meanings in common sense.

a. 15 theorem
b. BDDC
c. BIBO stability
d. Diagram

6. The _____ of a material is defined as its mass per unit volume. The symbol of _____ is ρ '>rho.)

Mathematically:

$$d = \frac{m}{V}$$

where:

d is the _____,
m is the mass,
V is the volume.

a. Density
b. BIBO stability
c. 15 theorem
d. BDDC

7. In mathematics, a probability _____ is a function that represents a probability distribution in terms of integrals.

Formally, a probability distribution has density f, if f is a non-negative Lebesgue-integrable function $\mathbb{R} \to \mathbb{R}$ such that the probability of the interval [a, b] is given by

$$\int_a^b f(x)\,dx$$

for any two numbers a and b. This implies that the total integral of f must be 1.

   a. Factorial moment generating function
   b. Density function
   c. 15 theorem
   d. BDDC

8. In mathematics, a _____ (pdf) is a function that represents a probability distribution in terms of integrals.

Formally, a probability distribution has density f, if f is a non-negative Lebesgue-integrable function $\mathbb{R} \to \mathbb{R}$ such that the probability of the interval [a, b] is given by

$$\int_a^b f(x)\,dx$$

for any two numbers a and b. This implies that the total integral of f must be 1.

   a. BDDC
   b. Probability density function
   c. Factorial moment generating function
   d. 15 theorem

9. In mathematics, a (topological) _____ is defined as follows: let I be an interval of real numbers (i.e. a non-empty connected subset of $\mathbb{R}$); then a _____ γ is a continuous mapping $\gamma : I \to X$, where X is a topological space. The _____ γ is said to be simple if it is injective, i.e. if for all x, y in I, we have $\gamma(x) = \gamma(y) \implies x = y$. If I is a closed bounded interval $[a, b]$, we also allow the possibility $\gamma(a) = \gamma(b)$ (this convention makes it possible to talk about closed simple _____.)
   a. Tractrix
   b. Prolate cycloid
   c. Curve
   d. Closed curve

10. In probability theory and statistics, the _____ or just distribution function, completely describes the probability distribution of a real-valued random variable X. For every real number x, the _____ of X is given by

$$x \mapsto F_X(x) = \mathrm{P}(X \leq x),$$

where the right-hand side represents the probability that the random variable X takes on a value less than or equal to x. The probability that X lies in the interval (a, b] is therefore $F_X(b) - F_X(a)$ if a < b.

If treating several random variables X, Y, ...

a. 15 theorem
b. Cumulative distribution function
c. BIBO stability
d. BDDC

11. The _____ is an important family of continuous probability distributions, applicable in many fields. Each member of the family may be defined by two parameters, location and scale: the mean and variance respectively. The standard _____ is the _____ with a mean of zero and a variance of one.

a. Correlation
b. Moment
c. Normal distribution
d. Continuous random variable

12. In mathematics and its applications, a _____ system is a system for assigning an n-tuple of numbers or scalars to each point in an n-dimensional space. This concept is part of the theory of manifolds. 'Scalars' in many cases means real numbers, but, depending on context, can mean complex numbers or elements of some other commutative ring.

a. Coordinate
b. 15 theorem
c. Spherical coordinate system
d. Cylindrical coordinate system

13. In molecular kinetic theory in physics, a particle's _____ is a function of seven variables, $f(x,y,z,t;v_x,v_y,v_z)$, which gives the number of particles per unit volume in phase space. It is the number of particles having approximately the velocity (v_x,v_y,v_z) near the place (x,y,z) and time (t). The usual normalization of the _____ is

$$n(x,y,z,t) = \int f\, dv_x\, dv_y\, dv_z$$

$$N(t) = \int n\, dx\, dy\, dz$$

Here, N is the total number of particles and n is the number density of particles - the number of particles per unit volume, or the density divided by the mass of individual particles.

   a. BIBO stability
   b. Distribution function
   c. BDDC
   d. 15 theorem

14. The _____ specifies the relationship between the two central operations of calculus, differentiation and integration.

The first part of the theorem, sometimes called the first _____, shows that an indefinite integration can be reversed by a differentiation.

The second part, sometimes called the second _____, allows one to compute the definite integral of a function by using any one of its infinitely many antiderivatives.

   a. Periodic function
   b. Fundamental Theorem of Calculus
   c. Limits of integration
   d. Leibniz formula

15. In probability theory, a probability distribution is called continuous if its cumulative distribution function is continuous. This is equivalent to saying that for random variables X with the distribution in question, Pr[X = a] = 0 for all real numbers a, i.e.: the probability that X attains the value a is zero, for any number a. If the distribution of X is continuous then X is called a _____.

   a. Probability
   b. Poisson distribution
   c. Standard deviation
   d. Continuous random variable

Chapter 6. Probability Theory and Descriptive Statistics

16. In mathematics and statistics, the _____ of a list of numbers is the sum of all of the list divided by the number of items in the list. If the list is a statistical population, then the mean of that population is called a population mean. If the list is a statistical sample, we call the resulting statistic a sample mean.

   a. ACTRAN
   b. Arithmetic mean
   c. ALGOR
   d. AUSM

17. In probability theory and statistics, the _____ (or expectation value or mean and for continuous random variables with a density function it is the probability density -weighted integral of the possible values.

   The term '_____' can be misleading.

   a. Expected value
   b. AUSM
   c. ACTRAN
   d. ALGOR

18. In mathematics, a _____ is a method for approximating the total area underneath a curve on a graph, otherwise known as an integral. It may also be used to define the integration operation.

   Consider a function $f: D \rightarrow R$, where D is a subset of the real numbers R, and let $I = [a, b]$ be a closed interval contained in D. A finite set of points $\{x_0, x_1, x_2, ... x_n\}$ such that $a = x_0 < x_1 < x_2 ... < x_n = b$ creates a partition

   $$P = \{[x_0, x_1], [x_1, x_2], ... [x_{n-1}, x_n]\}$$

   of I.

   a. Riemann sum
   b. Signed measure
   c. Risch algorithm
   d. Solid of revolution

19. The _____ of a system of particles is a specific point at which, for many purposes, the system's mass behaves as if it were concentrated. The _____ is a function only of the positions and masses of the particles that comprise the system. In the case of a rigid body, the position of its _____ is fixed in relation to the object (but not necessarily in contact with it.)

a. Simple harmonic motion
b. 15 theorem
c. Center of mass
d. Fundamental lemma in the calculus of variations

20. In probability theory and statistics, a _____ is described as the number separating the higher half of a sample, a population from the lower half. The _____ of a finite list of numbers can be found by arranging all the observations from lowest value to highest value and picking the middle one. If there is an even number of observations, the _____ is not unique, so one often takes the mean of the two middle values.
a. Geometric mean
b. Correlation
c. Moment
d. Median

21. The _____, in mathematics, is a type of mean or average, which indicates the central tendency or typical value of a set of numbers. It is similar to the arithmetic mean, which is what most people think of with the word 'average,' except that instead of adding the set of numbers and then dividing the sum by the count of numbers in the set, n, the numbers are multiplied and then the nth root of the resulting product is taken.

For instance, the _____ of two numbers, say 2 and 8, is just the square root (i.e., the second root) of their product, 16, which is 4.

a. Continuous random variable
b. Standard deviation
c. Normal distribution
d. Geometric mean

22. In mathematics, the _____ of a function is the set of all 'output' values produced by that function. Sometimes it is called the image, or more precisely, the image of the domain of the function. If a function is a surjection then its _____ is equal to its codomain.
a. Surjective
b. Range
c. Constant function
d. Piecewise-defined function

23. In statistics, _____ is a simple measure of the variability or dispersion of a data set. A low _____ indicates that all of the data points are very close to the same value (the mean), while high _____ indicates that the data is 'spread out' over a large range of values.

For example, the average height for adult men in the United States is about 70 inches, with a _____ of around 3 inches.

   a. Correlation
   b. Standard deviation
   c. Continuous random variable
   d. Poisson distribution

24. In differential calculus, an inflection point, or _____ (or inflexion) is a point on a curve at which the curvature changes sign. The curve changes from being concave upwards (positive curvature) to concave downwards (negative curvature), or vice versa. If one imagines driving a vehicle along the curve, it is a point at which the steering-wheel is momentarily 'straight', being turned from left to right or vice versa.
   a. Derivative of a constant
   b. Lin-Tsien equation
   c. Logarithmic derivative
   d. Point of inflection

25. In mathematics, _____ and minima, known collectively as extrema, are the largest value (maximum) or smallest value (minimum), that a function takes in a point either within a given neighbourhood (local extremum) or on the function domain in its entirety (global extremum.)

Throughout, a point refers to an input (x), while a value refers to an output (y): one distinguishing between the maximum value and the point (or points) at which it occurs.

A real-valued function f defined on the real line is said to have a local maximum point at the point x^*, if there exists some $\varepsilon > 0$, such that $f(x^*) \geq f(x)$ when $|x - x^*| < \varepsilon$.

   a. Racetrack principle
   b. Related rates
   c. Maxima
   d. Leibniz formula

26. In mathematics, a _____ is a constant multiplicative factor of a certain object. For example, in the expression $9x^2$, the _____ of x^2 is 9.

The object can be such things as a variable, a vector, a function, etc.

a. Coefficient
b. Binomial type
c. Degree of the polynomial
d. Resultant

Chapter 7. Probability Models

1. A _____ is the location at which two or more bones make contact. They are constructed to allow movement and provide mechanical support, and are classified structurally and functionally. Depiction of an intervertebral disk, a cartilaginous _____. Diagram of a synovial (diarthrosis) _____.

Joints are mainly classified structurally and functionally.

   a. BDDC
   b. BIBO stability
   c. 15 theorem
   d. Joint

2. _____ is a way of expressing knowledge or belief that an event will occur or has occurred. In mathematics the concept has been given an exact meaning in _____ theory, that is used extensively in such areas of study as mathematics, statistics, finance, gambling, science, and philosophy to draw conclusions about the likelihood of potential events and the underlying mechanics of complex systems.

The word _____ does not have a consistent direct definition.

   a. Normal distribution
   b. Discrete probability distributions
   c. Linear regression
   d. Probability

3. In probability theory and statistics, _____ indicates the strength and direction of a linear relationship between two random variables. That is in contrast with the usage of the term in colloquial speech, denoting any relationship, not necessarily linear. In general statistical usage, _____ or co-relation refers to the departure of two random variables from independence.
   a. Correlation
   b. Continuous random variable
   c. Standard deviation
   d. Geometric mean

4. _____ is a type of motion in which the velocity of an object changes equal amounts in equal time periods. An example of an object having _____ would be a ball rolling down a ramp. The object picks up velocity as it goes down the ramp with equal changes in time.
   a. ALGOR
   b. Uniform Acceleration
   c. AUSM
   d. ACTRAN

Chapter 7. Probability Models

5. In acoustics and telecommunication, a _____ of a wave is a component frequency of the signal that is an integer multiple of the fundamental frequency. For example, if the fundamental frequency is f, the harmonics have frequencies f, 2f, 3f, 4f, etc. The harmonics have the property that they are all periodic at the fundamental frequency, therefore the sum of harmonics is also periodic at that frequency.
   a. BIBO stability
   b. 15 theorem
   c. BDDC
   d. Harmonic

6. In probability theory and statistics, the _____ (or expectation value or mean and for continuous random variables with a density function it is the probability density -weighted integral of the possible values.

The term '_____' can be misleading.

   a. AUSM
   b. Expected value
   c. ACTRAN
   d. ALGOR

7. In elementary algebra, a _____ is a polynomial with two terms--the sum of two monomials--often bound by parenthesis or brackets when operated upon. It is the simplest kind of polynomial other than monomials.

- The _____ $a^2 - b^2$ can be factored as the product of two other binomials:

    $a^2 - b^2 = (a + b)(a - b.)$

    This is a special case of the more general formula: $a^{n+1} - b^{n+1} = (a - b) \sum_{k=0}^{n} a^k b^{n-k}$.

- The product of a pair of linear binomials (ax + b) and (cx + d) is:

    $(ax + b)(cx + d) = acx^2 + axd + bcx + bd.$

- A _____ raised to the nth power, represented as

    $(a + b)^n$

    can be expanded by means of the _____ theorem or, equivalently, using Pascal's triangle. Taking a simple example, the perfect square _____ $(p + q)^2$ can be found by squaring the first digit, adding twice the product of the first and second digit and finally adding the square of the second digit, to give $p^2 + 2pq + q^2$.

a. Partial fractions
b. Multinomial theorem
c. Binomial
d. Completing the square

8. In probability theory and statistics, the _____ is the discrete probability distribution of the number of successes in a sequence of n independent yes/no experiments, each of which yields success with probability p. Such a success/failure experiment is also called a Bernoulli experiment or Bernoulli trial. In fact, when n = 1, the _____ is a Bernoulli distribution.
   a. Median
   b. Linear regression
   c. Probability
   d. Binomial distribution

9. In mathematics, the _____ of a non-negative integer n, denoted by n!, is the product of all positive integers less than or equal to n. For example,

$$5! = 1 \times 2 \times 3 \times 4 \times 5 = 120$$

and

$$6! = 1 \times 2 \times 3 \times 4 \times 5 \times 6 = 720.$$

The notation n! was introduced by Christian Kramp in 1808.

The _____ function is formally defined by

$$n! = \prod_{k=1}^{n} k \qquad \forall n \in \mathbb{N}$$

or recursively defined by

$$n! = \begin{cases} n \leq 1 & 1 \\ n > 1 & n(n-1)! \end{cases} \qquad \forall n \in \mathbb{N}.$$

Both of the above definitions incorporate the instance

$$0! = 1$$

as an instance of the fact that the product of no numbers at all is 1.

   a. BDDC
   b. Constraint counting
   c. 15 theorem
   d. Factorial

10. In mathematics, the _____ $\binom{n}{k}$ is the coefficient of the x^k term in the polynomial expansion of the binomial power $(1 + x)^n$.

In combinatorics, $\binom{n}{k}$ is interpreted as the number of k-element subsets (the k-combinations) of an n-element set, that is the number of ways that k things can be 'chosen' from a set of n things. Hence, $\binom{n}{k}$ is often read as 'n choose k' and is called the choose function of n and k.

   a. BDDC
   b. 15 theorem
   c. Factorial
   d. Binomial coefficient

11. In mathematics, a _____ is a constant multiplicative factor of a certain object. For example, in the expression $9x^2$, the _____ of x^2 is 9.

The object can be such things as a variable, a vector, a function, etc.

   a. Degree of the polynomial
   b. Binomial type
   c. Resultant
   d. Coefficient

12. In a totally ordered set all elements are mutually comparable, so such a set can have at most one minimal element and at most one maximal element. Then, due to mutual comparability, the minimal element will also be the least element and the maximal element will also be the greatest element. Thus in a totally ordered set we can simply use the terms minimum and _____.

a. Leibniz rule
b. Maximum
c. Racetrack principle
d. Nth term

13. In probability theory, the _____ is a generalization of the binomial distribution.

The binomial distribution is the probability distribution of the number of 'successes' in n independent Bernoulli trials, with the same probability of 'success' on each trial. In a _____, the analog of the Bernoulli distribution is the categorical distribution, where each trial results in exactly one of some fixed finite number k of possible outcomes, with probabilities $p_1, ..., p_k$ (so that $p_i \geq 0$ for i = 1, ..., k and $\sum_{i=1}^{k} p_i = 1$), and there are n independent trials.

a. Multinomial distribution
b. BDDC
c. Negative binomial distribution
d. 15 theorem

14. In probability and statistics the _____ is a discrete probability distribution. It arises as the probability distribution of the number of failures in a sequence of Bernoulli trials needed to get a specified (non-random) number of successes. If one throws a die repeatedly until the third time a '1' appears, then the probability distribution of the number of non-'1's that appear before the third '1' is a _____.

a. 15 theorem
b. Multinomial distribution
c. BDDC
d. Negative binomial distribution

15. In probability theory and statistics, the _____ is a discrete probability distribution that expresses the probability of a number of events occurring in a fixed period of time if these events occur with a known average rate and independently of the time since the last event. The _____ can also be used for the number of events in other specified intervals such as distance, area or volume.

The distribution was discovered by Siméon-Denis Poisson (1781-1840) and published, together with his probability theory, in 1838 in his work Recherches sur la probabilité des jugements en matières criminelles et matière civile ('Research on the Probability of Judgments in Criminal and Civil Matters'.)

Chapter 7. Probability Models

a. Median
b. Discrete probability distributions
c. Probability
d. Poisson distribution

16. _____ is any physical or virtual entity that is owned by an individual or jointly by a group of individuals. An owner of _____ has the right to consume, sell, rent, mortgage, transfer and exchange his or her _____. Important widely-recognized types of _____ include real _____, personal _____ (other physical possessions), and intellectual _____ (rights over artistic creations, inventions, etc.), although the latter is not always as widely recognized or enforced.
   a. 15 theorem
   b. BDDC
   c. BIBO stability
   d. Property

17. The _____ is an important family of continuous probability distributions, applicable in many fields. Each member of the family may be defined by two parameters, location and scale: the mean and variance respectively. The standard _____ is the _____ with a mean of zero and a variance of one.
   a. Continuous random variable
   b. Moment
   c. Normal distribution
   d. Correlation

18. The _____ of a material is defined as its mass per unit volume. The symbol of _____ is ρ '>rho.)

Mathematically:

$$d = \frac{m}{V}$$

where:

      d is the _____,
      m is the mass,
      V is the volume.

a. BIBO stability
b. 15 theorem
c. BDDC
d. Density

19. In mathematics, a probability _____ is a function that represents a probability distribution in terms of integrals.

Formally, a probability distribution has density f, if f is a non-negative Lebesgue-integrable function $\mathbb{R} \longrightarrow \mathbb{R}$ such that the probability of the interval [a, b] is given by

$$\int_a^b f(x)\,dx$$

for any two numbers a and b. This implies that the total integral of f must be 1.

a. Density function
b. Factorial moment generating function
c. BDDC
d. 15 theorem

20. In mathematics, a _____ (pdf) is a function that represents a probability distribution in terms of integrals.

Formally, a probability distribution has density f, if f is a non-negative Lebesgue-integrable function $\mathbb{R} \longrightarrow \mathbb{R}$ such that the probability of the interval [a, b] is given by

$$\int_a^b f(x)\,dx$$

for any two numbers a and b. This implies that the total integral of f must be 1.

a. BDDC
b. 15 theorem
c. Probability density function
d. Factorial moment generating function

21. In mathematics, an _____ is a function that always returns the same value that was used as its argument. In terms of equations, the function is given by f = x.

Formally, if M is a set, the _____ f on M is defined to be that function with domain and codomain M which satisfies

f = x for all elements x in M.

a. Onto
b. Identity function
c. One-to-one
d. One-to-one function

22. In mathematics, the concept of a '_____' is used to describe the behavior of a function as its argument or input either 'gets close' to some point, or as the argument becomes arbitrarily large; or the behavior of a sequence's elements as their index increases indefinitely. Limits are used in calculus and other branches of mathematical analysis to define derivatives and continuity.

In formulas, _____ is usually abbreviated as lim

a. 15 theorem
b. BIBO stability
c. Limit
d. BDDC

23. In probability theory and statistics, the _____ is a two-parameter family of continuous probability distributions. It has a scale parameter θ and a shape parameter k. If k is an integer then the distribution represents the sum of k independent exponentially distributed random variables, each of which has a mean of θ (which is equivalent to a rate parameter of $θ^{-1}$) .

a. BDDC
b. Gamma distribution
c. Nakagami distribution
d. 15 theorem

24. The _____, in mathematics, is a type of mean or average, which indicates the central tendency or typical value of a set of numbers. It is similar to the arithmetic mean, which is what most people think of with the word 'average,' except that instead of adding the set of numbers and then dividing the sum by the count of numbers in the set, n, the numbers are multiplied and then the nth root of the resulting product is taken.

For instance, the _____ of two numbers, say 2 and 8, is just the square root (i.e., the second root) of their product, 16, which is 4.

Chapter 7. Probability Models

a. Continuous random variable
b. Standard deviation
c. Geometric mean
d. Normal distribution

25. In probability theory and statistics, the _____ or just distribution function, completely describes the probability distribution of a real-valued random variable X. For every real number x, the _____ of X is given by

$$x \mapsto F_X(x) = \mathrm{P}(X \leq x),$$

where the right-hand side represents the probability that the random variable X takes on a value less than or equal to x. The probability that X lies in the interval (a, b] is therefore $F_X(b) - F_X(a)$ if a < b.

If treating several random variables X, Y, ...

a. BIBO stability
b. 15 theorem
c. Cumulative distribution function
d. BDDC

26. In molecular kinetic theory in physics, a particle's _____ is a function of seven variables, $f(x,y,z,t;v_x,v_y,v_z)$, which gives the number of particles per unit volume in phase space. It is the number of particles having approximately the velocity (v_x,v_y,v_z) near the place (x,y,z) and time (t). The usual normalization of the _____ is

$$n(x, y, z, t) = \int f \, dv_x \, dv_y \, dv_z$$

$$N(t) = \int n \, dx \, dy \, dz$$

Here, N is the total number of particles and n is the number density of particles - the number of particles per unit volume, or the density divided by the mass of individual particles.

a. BIBO stability
b. BDDC
c. 15 theorem
d. Distribution function

Chapter 7. Probability Models

27. The _____ is a polynomial mapping of degree 2, often cited as an archetypal example of how complex, chaotic behaviour can arise from very simple non-linear dynamical equations. The map was popularized in a seminal 1976 paper by the biologist Robert May, in part as a discrete-time demographic model analogous to the logistic equation first created by Pierre François Verhulst. Mathematically, the _____ is written

$$(1) \quad x_{n+1} = rx_n(1 - x_n)$$

where:

x_n is a number between zero and one, and represents the population at year n, and hence x_0 represents the initial population (at year 0)

r is a positive number, and represents a combined rate for reproduction and starvation.

a. 15 theorem
b. BDDC
c. BIBO stability
d. Logistic map

Chapter 8. Introduction to Statistical Reasoning

1. In probability theory and statistics, a _____ is described as the number separating the higher half of a sample, a population from the lower half. The _____ of a finite list of numbers can be found by arranging all the observations from lowest value to highest value and picking the middle one. If there is an even number of observations, the _____ is not unique, so one often takes the mean of the two middle values.

   a. Correlation
   b. Moment
   c. Geometric mean
   d. Median

2. In mathematics, the concept of a '_____' is used to describe the behavior of a function as its argument or input either 'gets close' to some point, or as the argument becomes arbitrarily large; or the behavior of a sequence's elements as their index increases indefinitely. Limits are used in calculus and other branches of mathematical analysis to define derivatives and continuity.

   In formulas, _____ is usually abbreviated as lim

   a. BDDC
   b. BIBO stability
   c. Limit
   d. 15 theorem

3. In probability theory and statistics, the _____ (or expectation value or mean and for continuous random variables with a density function it is the probability density -weighted integral of the possible values.

   The term '_____' can be misleading.

   a. AUSM
   b. ACTRAN
   c. ALGOR
   d. Expected value

4. In statistics, _____ is a simple measure of the variability or dispersion of a data set. A low _____ indicates that all of the data points are very close to the same value (the mean), while high _____ indicates that the data is 'spread out' over a large range of values.

   For example, the average height for adult men in the United States is about 70 inches, with a _____ of around 3 inches.

Chapter 8. Introduction to Statistical Reasoning

a. Continuous random variable
b. Poisson distribution
c. Standard deviation
d. Correlation

5. In elementary algebra, a _____ is a polynomial with two terms--the sum of two monomials--often bound by parenthesis or brackets when operated upon. It is the simplest kind of polynomial other than monomials.

- The _____ $a^2 - b^2$ can be factored as the product of two other binomials:

    $a^2 - b^2 = (a + b)(a - b.)$

    This is a special case of the more general formula:

    $$a^{n+1} - b^{n+1} = (a - b) \sum_{k=0}^{n} a^k b^{n-k}$$

- The product of a pair of linear binomials (ax + b) and (cx + d) is:

    $(ax + b)(cx + d) = acx^2 + axd + bcx + bd.$

- A _____ raised to the nth power, represented as

    $(a + b)^n$
    can be expanded by means of the _____ theorem or, equivalently, using Pascal's triangle. Taking a simple example, the perfect square _____ $(p + q)^2$ can be found by squaring the :first digit, adding twice the product of the first and second digit and finally adding the square of the second digit, to give $p^2 + 2pq + q^2$.

a. Binomial
b. Completing the square
c. Multinomial theorem
d. Partial fractions

6. _____ is usually defined as the activity of using and developing computer technology, computer hardware and software. It is the computer-specific part of information technology. Computer science (or _____ science) is the study and the science of the theoretical foundations of information and computation and their implementation and application in computer systems.
   a. BIBO stability
   b. 15 theorem
   c. BDDC
   d. Computing

7. The _____ is an important family of continuous probability distributions, applicable in many fields. Each member of the family may be defined by two parameters, location and scale: the mean and variance respectively. The standard _____ is the _____ with a mean of zero and a variance of one.
   a. Moment
   b. Normal distribution
   c. Continuous random variable
   d. Correlation

8. _____ is any physical or virtual entity that is owned by an individual or jointly by a group of individuals. An owner of _____ has the right to consume, sell, rent, mortgage, transfer and exchange his or her _____. Important widely-recognized types of _____ include real _____, personal _____ (other physical possessions), and intellectual _____ (rights over artistic creations, inventions, etc.), although the latter is not always as widely recognized or enforced.
   a. 15 theorem
   b. BDDC
   c. Property
   d. BIBO stability

9. In statistics, _____ is a form of regression analysis in which the relationship between one or more independent variables and another variable, called dependent variable, is modeled by a least squares function, called _____ equation. This function is a linear combination of one or more model parameters, called regression coefficients. A _____ equation with one independent variable represents a straight line.
   a. Linear regression
   b. Probability
   c. Correlation
   d. Standard deviation

10. In mathematics, a _____ is a constant multiplicative factor of a certain object. For example, in the expression $9x^2$, the _____ of x^2 is 9.

The object can be such things as a variable, a vector, a function, etc.

   a. Binomial type
   b. Degree of the polynomial
   c. Coefficient
   d. Resultant

11. In mathematics, a _____ of a function of several variables is its derivative with respect to one of those variables with the others held constant (as opposed to the total derivative, in which all variables are allowed to vary.) Partial derivatives are useful in vector calculus and differential geometry.

The _____ of a function f with respect to the variable x is written as f'_x, $\partial_x f$, or $\partial f/\partial x$.

a. Jacobian
b. Partial derivative
c. Level curve
d. Differentiation operator

12. _____ is used to describe the steepness, incline, gradient, or grade of a straight line. A higher _____ value indicates a steeper incline. The _____ is defined as the ratio of the 'rise' divided by the 'run' between two points on a line, or in other words, the ratio of the altitude change to the horizontal distance between any two points on the line.

a. Sequence
b. 15 theorem
c. Y-intercept
d. Slope

13. In calculus, a branch of mathematics, the _____ is a measurement of how a function changes when its input changes. Loosely speaking, a _____ can be thought of as how much a quantity is changing at some given point. For example, the _____ of the position (or distance) of a vehicle with respect to time is the instantaneous velocity (respectively, instantaneous speed) at which the vehicle is traveling.

The process of finding a _____ is called differentiation. The fundamental theorem of calculus states that differentiation is the reverse process to integration.

a. Derivative
b. Semi-differentiability
c. Bounded function
d. Stationary phase approximation

14. The method of _____ or ordinary _____ is used to solve overdetermined systems. _____ is often applied in statistical contexts, particularly regression analysis.

_____ can be interpreted as a method of fitting data. The best fit in the _____ sense is that instance of the model for which the sum of squared residuals has its least value, a residual being the difference between an observed value and the value given by the model.

Chapter 8. Introduction to Statistical Reasoning

   a. Least squares
   b. BDDC
   c. 15 theorem
   d. BIBO stability

15. In probability theory and statistics, _____ indicates the strength and direction of a linear relationship between two random variables. That is in contrast with the usage of the term in colloquial speech, denoting any relationship, not necessarily linear. In general statistical usage, _____ or co-relation refers to the departure of two random variables from independence.
   a. Standard deviation
   b. Geometric mean
   c. Correlation
   d. Continuous random variable

16. In calculus, the _____ is a method of finding the derivative of a function that is the quotient of two other functions for which derivatives exist.

If the function one wishes to differentiate, f(x), can be written as

$$f(x) = \frac{g(x)}{h(x)}$$

and h(x) ≠ 0, then the rule states that the derivative of g(x) / h(x) is equal to:

$$\frac{d}{dx}f(x) = f'(x) = \frac{g'(x)h(x) - g(x)h'(x)}{[h(x)]^2}.$$

Or, more precisely, if all x in some open set containing the number a satisfy h(x) ≠ 0; and g'(a) and h'(a) both exist; then, f'(a) exists as well and:

$$f'(a) = \frac{g'(a)h(a) - g(a)h'(a)}{[h(a)]^2}.$$

Chapter 8. Introduction to Statistical Reasoning

The derivative of (4x − 2) / (x² + 1) is:

$$\frac{d}{dx}\left[\frac{(4x-2)}{x^2+1}\right] = \frac{(x^2+1)(4)-(4x-2)(2x)}{(x^2+1)^2}$$

$$= \frac{(4x^2+4)-(8x^2-4x)}{(x^2+1)^2} = \frac{-4x^2+4x+4}{(x^2+1)^2}$$

In the example above, the choices

g(x) = 4x − 2
h(x) = x² + 1

were made. Analogously, the derivative of sin(x) / x² (when x ≠ 0) is:

$$\frac{\cos(x)x^2 - \sin(x)2x}{x^4}$$

Another example is:

$$f(x) = \frac{2x^2}{x^3}$$

whereas g(x) = 2x² and h(x) = x³, and g'(x) = 4x and h'(x) = 3x².

a. Differentiation rules
b. Constant factor rule in differentiation
c. Reciprocal Rule
d. Quotient rule

ANSWER KEY

Chapter 1
1. d   2. c   3. b   4. c   5. b   6. d   7. d   8. d   9. c   10. c
11. d   12. a   13. c   14. b   15. b   16. b   17. b   18. d   19. c   20. b
21. c   22. a   23. d   24. d   25. d   26. d   27. b   28. d   29. d   30. a
31. b   32. d   33. d   34. d   35. d   36. a   37. b   38. b   39. b   40. b
41. d   42. a   43. d   44. a

Chapter 2
1. d   2. a   3. a   4. a   5. d   6. d   7. a   8. a   9. d   10. c
11. d   12. c   13. d   14. d   15. b   16. d   17. a   18. b   19. c   20. d
21. d   22. b   23. c   24. c   25. a   26. a   27. b   28. d   29. a   30. b
31. d   32. d   33. d   34. d   35. d   36. c   37. d   38. d   39. a   40. d
41. b   42. c   43. c   44. b   45. b   46. b   47. d

Chapter 3
1. d   2. a   3. d   4. c   5. a   6. a   7. c   8. c   9. d   10. d
11. c   12. b   13. d   14. d   15. d   16. a   17. b   18. c   19. d   20. c
21. d   22. b   23. d   24. a   25. d   26. c   27. a   28. d   29. d   30. d
31. a   32. d   33. d   34. d   35. b   36. d   37. b   38. d   39. a   40. d

Chapter 4
1. c   2. b   3. d   4. d   5. d   6. c   7. c   8. d   9. d   10. c
11. a   12. a   13. d   14. d   15. d   16. d   17. d   18. d   19. c   20. a
21. d   22. b   23. d   24. d   25. d   26. d   27. c   28. a   29. a   30. b
31. d   32. d   33. d   34. d   35. b   36. d   37. b   38. d

Chapter 5
1. a   2. d   3. b   4. a   5. c   6. d   7. d   8. d   9. d   10. d
11. a   12. d   13. a   14. a   15. d   16. b   17. d   18. d   19. a   20. c

Chapter 6
1. d   2. a   3. d   4. b   5. d   6. a   7. b   8. b   9. c   10. b
11. c   12. a   13. b   14. b   15. d   16. b   17. a   18. a   19. c   20. d
21. d   22. b   23. b   24. d   25. c   26. a

Chapter 7
1. d   2. d   3. a   4. b   5. d   6. b   7. c   8. d   9. d   10. d
11. d   12. b   13. a   14. d   15. d   16. d   17. c   18. d   19. a   20. c
21. b   22. c   23. b   24. c   25. c   26. d   27. d

Chapter 8
1. d   2. c   3. d   4. c   5. a   6. d   7. b   8. c   9. a   10. c
11. b   12. d   13. a   14. a   15. c   16. d

www.ingramcontent.com/pod-product-compliance
Lightning Source LLC
Chambersburg PA
CBHW081847230426
43669CB00018B/2849